Terror in Tribeca / Murderer's Mitigation:

Sayfullo Saipov in the SDNY

By Matthew Russell Lee

Inner City Press

Halloween 2017 to March 13, 2023

Halloween in lower Manhattan means a parade in Greenwich Village; on October 31, 2017 there were bicyclists on the West Side Highway bike path, many of them tourists, from Argentina and Belgium and elsewhere.

Then there was a motorist from Uzbekistan. He'd been a truck driver in Ohio, and here in the tri-state area he drove an Uber. Today he drove a pick-up truck rented from Home Depot. He'd rented one days before, as a trial run. This afternoon, Halloween, it was no longer a trial run. And no one knew then it would turn into a trial.

* * *

Sayfullo Saipov had been in the Metropolitan Correctional Center for more than two years when, on November 18, 2019, he was brought through the third story walkway into a large courtroom in 40 Foley Square. When first read his Miranda rights in the hospital after he was shot but not killed by police, Saipov had asked to hang the ISIS flag on his wall. Now he demanded of the judge, Vernon S. Broderick, what about the thousands of Muslims killed by the United States?

In the courtroom gallery, Kurt Wheelock was taking notes. He had been told he couldn't use his phone to live-tweet what was being said. He'd been thrown out of the United Nations for using social media to expose the corruption of UN Secretary-General Antonio Guterres, who took selfies with terrorists. So here Kurt played by the rules. When the proceeding was over, he ran out onto Foley Square and livestreamed on Periscope. It was the beginning of a story, a story that might end in death.

But before it did, the judge tried to exclude the Press from the Saipov courtroom. Kurt

Wheelock filed a fast and first opposition, and unlike at the UN the exclusion was reversed.

See, e.g., Feb 21, 2023, El Pais (Spain), "Judge bars public from court in NYC bike path terror trial," "Matthew Russell Lee of the Inner City Press noted that the presence of the media was "particularly important in capital cases," https://english.elpais.com/usa/2023-02-21/judge-bars-public-from-court-in-nyc-bike-path-terror-trial.html & https://thehill.com/homenews/ap/ap-u-s-news/ap-judge-bars-public-from-court-in-nyc-bike-path-terror-trial/ & https://www.courttv.com/news/judge-bars-public-from-court-in-nyc-bike-path-terror-trial/

The difference, perhaps, was that unlike as to the United Nations, here some law applied, some binding law. On this Kurt as before consulted with his right-hand man Michael Randall Long. Long had moved his law office from atop Ali Baba's fruit market on Worth Street, which had unceremoniously closed at the tail end of the COVID lockdowns, over to Park Row with its history both of journalism and of jails.

The Metropolitan Correctional Center at 150 Park Row was of particular interest to Michael Randall Long. It was where Jeffrey Epstein had tried to commit suicide - twice, the Bureau of Prisons authorities said - and where death penalty candidate Nicholas Tartaglione, Epstein's cellmate during the first attempt, had tried to get the video.

The video, BOP said, had been destroyed. And then Attorney General Merrick Garland unlike for Saipov took the death penalty off the table for Tartaglione, an ex-cop charged with the murder of four in SDNY. Long had an interest in the Tartaglione trial set to begin in the District's White Plains courthouse after Saipov's two-phase trial. But could he get up there?

Long listened to what Kurt told him, sure, and what Kurt tweeted. But he also looked up the actual transcripts. From November 18, 2019:

THE DEFENDANT: "These things happen as the result and response to multiple occasions when Muslims all over the world, the women and the kids, are dying under the bombs of the American government... you're judging me for the eight people killed, and you're not judging the prosecution when the thousands and thousands of Muslims are dying all over the world. Why are you judging me and not judging those who killed thousands and millions of Muslims all over the world?"

THE COURT: "I am here to preside over your trial. I am not going to decide your guilt or your innocence. I'm not going to decide an issue of penalty, so I'm more like a referee."

Long told Kurt, and through him others, that Judge Broderick's disclaiming any role in the penalty wasn't quite true. Later in the trial(s), in the penalty phase when a jury question asked if they could consider lethal injection, Broderick remarked on the record that since New York State did not have the death penalty, it would be he, as the judge, who would decide the method of execution.

That was only indirectly true, Long distinguished. Under the Federal Death Penalty Act, the District Judge presiding over trials in states without the capital crimes would designate another state's methodology to follow, a state that did have the death penalty.

In the final days of Trump, Indiana had been chosen, since the Land of Pence hosted FCI Terre Haute and the federal death row. Of course there would be litigation. There was always litigation, right to the end. A final look and memo by the Supreme Court's death clerk, Danny Bickell or Cynthia Rapp; a final midnight perusal by at least one Justice - God help the condemned man who got Sam Alito, at least if the issue was the method or chemical cocktail of execution.

It would be different under Justice Sotomayor, coming from the Soundview housing projects in the Bronx which Kurt knew well, first from when he lived in the Boogie Down and now through SDNY cases spanning from Sex Money Murder to the millennial proliferation of gangs. If it came to that. Kurt thanked Michael Randall Long and tucked the legal factoids away. He tried not to be pedantic but these might come in handy.

And looking back into the docket to the time before he arrived at the court, fresh from being thrown out of the UN, Kurt found a strange docket entry of November 9, 2017, SEALED DOCUMENT as to JOHN DOE (signed by Magistrate Judge Henry B. Pitman on 11/9/17 (dif) [1:17-mj-081770-UA] [Entered: 11/09/2017]

See, https://www.courtlistener.com/docket/6279593/united-states-v-saipov/?filed_after=&filed_before=&entry_gte=&entry_lte=&order_by=asc#entry-7

What was it? Who was John Doe?

That Sayfullo Saipov was charged under the Federal Death Penalty Act itself had a history. Starting in 1963, federal executions stopped.

In 1994, Congress enacted the Federal Death Penalty Act, 18 USC 3591-3598.

Then Oklahoma City bomber Timothy McVeigh waived all his appeals and was put to death in Terre Haute, Indiana. Trump after calling for Saipov to be killed managed to schedule five executions for his waning months.

Saipov's Federal Defenders filed papers zeroing in on Trump's pro death penalties tweets. But as the Federal Defenders pointed out, "in nearly identical circumstance, when in 1995 the President and Attorney General public commented during the investigation of the Oklahoma City bombing that the perpetrator of the crime should receive the death penalty, a district court denied a request to strike the Attorney General's decision to strike the death penalty. See Nichols v. Reno, 931 F. Supp. 748, 751-52 (D. Colo. 1996)."

But why hadn't Joe Biden de-authorized the death penalty for Saipov? His Attorney General Merrick Garland - all such decisions went to the top of DOJ - declined to seek death for the mass shooting of Latinos in Texas. This case had many mysteries.

The Justice Manual set out the Capital Case Protocol, under which the US Attorney made a recommendation to the Capital Review Committee. JM Section 9-10.080. Defense counsel had to be given an opportunity to present reasons why the death penalty should not be sought - or here, should no longer be sought.

From the time, Kurt published:

SDNY COURTHOUSE, Nov 18, 2019 – Sayfullo Saipov faces a trial that may result in the death penalty for killing eight people with a van along the West Side Highway.

But at a court appearance on November 18 before U.S. District Court for the Southern District of New York Judge Vernon S. Broderick, after his Federal Defender inquired into Saipov receiving dental care, Saipov told Judge Broderick he had not right to judge him.

As Inner City Press recounted moments later outside the courthouse on Pericope here - any use of phones in the courtroom was prohibited - Saipov asked Broderick, What about the thousands or millions of Muslims killed by American bombs?

Judge Broderick replied, I am just the referee, it is the jury that will judge you. And it emerged, that jury might be anonymous and/or semi-sequestered.

Much of the November 20 conference, delayed by problems with the sound system for the Uzbek interpreter, concerned how the jury will be selected. Some 3000 questionnaires will be mailed out, asking potential jurors about hardship but not disclosing what the case is about.

Judge Broderick said, with response rates to such summons being being 30%, perhaps it was better to spring more information on the prospect once they were in court.

Federal Defender alluded to an "incident" in which unspeficied inappropriate language was used; Judge Broderick responded but left the issue murky. Then Saipov asked to speak, and did. The case is *US v. Saipov*, 17-cr-722 (Broderick).

The guy from the SDNY courthouse cafeteria, Cafe Lorenzo, kept asking Kurt Wheelock when the death penalty trial would "really get going," thinking it would lead to a spike in their dwindling sales.

It never did. Cafe Lorenzo was the one, Kurt quipped, facing the end.

* * * *

While in the UN, Kurt Wheelock had asked and written about Uzbekistan, and terrorism which the UN had yet to define despite raising big money off the buzzword, money mostly from Gulf states that themselves supported extremist groups when it suited them.

Uzbekistan on the other hand was a country of repression. This didn't stop UN Secretary General Antonio Guterres from praising the government, both in 2017 just before Saipov's rampage in New York, and again in 2022, on counter-terrorism no less:

"On March 2, 2022, the President of Uzbekistan Shavkat Mirziyoyev met with the United Nations Under-Secretary-General for Counter-Terrorism Vladimir Voronkov who conveyed to the President of Uzbekistan the sincere greetings and best wishes of the United Nations Secretary-General Antonio Guterres... multilateral events in the framework of the Resolution of the General Assembly of the UN «Education and religious tolerance» adopted on the initiative of Uzbekistan, to protect the youth from a harmful influence of ideas of extremism and terrorism."

Yeah.

The UN's hypocrisy on terrorism mirrored its selective answers on the death penalty. Daily during Saipov's trial Kurt Wheelock e-mail Guterres' spokesman Stephane Dujarric seeking the UNSG's position on the Administration seeking to kill Saipov. No answer. And no one they let in even asked.

During the trial, Kurt learned that Sayfullo Saipov's father had been detained in Uzbekistan after his son's West Side Highway deed. Saipov's Federal Defender sought to take depositions in Uzbekistan, stymied first by COVID then by that government's prohibitions.

The trial, then, kept getting pushed back, into 2023. This is that story.

Back to April 2020, as the COVID pandemic hit and spread:

...in April 2020 amid the Coronavirus pandemic Saipov wants at least weekly legal calls until legal visiting resumes in the MCC. The US has asked until April 10 to respond. Meanwhile on April 7 Inner City Press heard from another judge about a possible laptop link between the Attorneys Lounge in 500 Pearl Street and the MCC, here.

On April 19, 2020 Saipov's Federal Defender Annalisa Miron raised questions: "United States v. Saipov, (S1) 17 Cr. 722 (VSB) Dear Judge Broderick: We appreciate the Jury Clerk's provision of well-organized data responsive to our demand for grand jury records (ECF No. 218, Attachment # 1, Declaration of Jeffrey Martin), which was endorsed by the Court (ECF No. 294). We write to follow up on a few incomplete responses:

1. The data supplied only included the odd page numbers for the Jury Plan. Please provide the entire Jury Plan. (If any other information that was meant to be supplied has the same problem with copying, please supply the missing information.)

2. The Form AO-12 for the Foley Division was supplied. Because the Foley Division and the White Plains Division overlap geographically, the Form AO-12 for the White Plains Division 2013 Jury Wheel is requested.

3. The email included in Jury Exhibit #1 is partially obscured by a sticky note. Please supply the entire email.

4. The response to the request for the voter registration source list is "Available directly from Board of Elections". The voter registration used to create the Jury Wheel used to summon grand jurors in this case is not the current voter list available from the Board of Elections but rather a historical list supplied to the Court. Please supply the list received by the Court to create the 2013 Master Wheels.

5. The data supplied included Jury Exhibit #4 (persons selected as potential grand jurors), electronic file Pool 101170310, and the 2013 Master Jury Wheel (Wheel 04 spreadsheet). There are some inconsistencies between these files; please explain the discrepancies.

6. Some of the persons on Jury Exhibit #4 (persons selected as potential grand jurors) are not in Pool 101170310 and/or not in the 2013 Master Jury Wheel (Wheel 04 spreadsheet). What is the explanation for why these persons are on Jury Exhibit #4?

7. Some of the persons in Pool 101170310 are not in the 2013 Master Jury Wheel (Wheel 04 spreadsheet). What is the explanation for why these persons are listed in Pool 101170310? Needless to say, we understand if the Jury Clerk is unable to access the requested information until the courthouse fully re-opens."

"Needless to say." And to fully re-open the SDNY courthouse would take quite a while...

On April 23, 2020 U.S. District Court for the Southern District of New York Judge Vernon S. Broderick held a conference on the case, resulting in a decision to release the previously questioned jurors and start over, when it is possible. Inner City Press covered it.

Judge Broderick said that due to COVID, there will probably be no SDNY jury trials until the fall.

Federal Defender David Patton said he does not favor keeping the jury pool to which questionnaires were previously given. He said people's answers might have changed.

AUSA Amanda Houle said the government does not object to dismissing that pool.

Judge Broderick agreed, adding that their personal situation might have changed, as will have the timing of the trial, "perhaps some time next year."

Ms. Thomas said, "We'll leave a message that they no longer need to call, the usual discharge of the jury. With the thanks of the court, of course."

Judge Broderick was forward-looking: Once we start letting members of the public back into the courthouse, what actually needs to happen from each party's perspective, in terms of the openness of the court and of society, to move this forward? Travel from overseas, social distancing.... There with be communications from the Chief Judge, and from the governor about restrictions, or the Federal government.

Judge Broderick said, The next date in is June, tied to the day that the Chief Judge excludes Speedy Trial Act until. "We could extend that if needed," he concluded.

No one knew then how long the COVID shutdowns would continue...

During the lull Michael Randall Long subject to his own special measures looked into Saipov's formal Special Administrative Measures, even though labeled "Limited Official Use."

The SAMs were styled, like Joshua Schulte's, as a memo from the Attorney General to the Director of the Bureau of Prisons, Mark S. Inch. The memo noted that

"ISIS subsequently took credit for Saipov's attack. On or about November 2, 2017 ISIS publicly discussed the attack in "al-Naba," its weekly newsletter, stating that "[o]ne of the Islamic State soldiers in America attacked on Tuesday a number of crusaders on a street in New York City."

These people - they were crusaders?

Diego Enrique Angelini, Nicholas Cleves, Ann-Laure Decadt, Darren Drake, Ariel Erlij, Hernan Ferruchi, Hernan Diego Mendoza & Alejandro Damian Pagnucco

The point of reciting ISIS' claim of credit quickly became clear: "I find that there is a substantial risk that his communications or contacts with persons could result in death or serious bodily harm to persons...The inmate shall be permitted to visit only with his immediate family members."

Then, "The inmate shall not be permitted to speak, meet, correspond, or otherwise communicate with any member of representative of the news media in person, by telephone, by furnishing a recorded message, through the mail, his attorney or a third party, or other side."

As with Josh Schulte, about whom Kurt nonetheless wrote a booklet (Brutal Kangaroo: https://www.amazon.com/gp/product/B0B6G RHV6J) this would bar Kurt. But would it bar or hinder Michael Randall Long?

Litigation about the SAMs would result in a finding that Saipov's first learned counsel - a lawyer with death penalty experience -- David Stern must be recused from it, due to a conflict of interest. So, at least for the SAMs litigation period, David Ruhnke was appointed.

Later, the prosecutors would push to get access to the visitor logs.... The trial was set for October 8, 2019 - but it would not take place then, would not begin until 2023...

On October 8, 2020 the US acknowledged late production of discovery but made other arguments:

"Re: United States v. Sayfullo Habibullaevic Saipov, S1 17 Cr. 722 (VSB)

Dear Judge Broderick: We write in response to the defendant's September 24, 2020 letter concerning the Government's recent production of additional recorded statements involving Saipov (the "Defense Letter"). In November 2018, the Government produced to the defense 683 telephone calls, 135 text messages, and three emails involving Saipov that the Federal Bureau of Investigation had collected in separate terrorism investigations pursuant to classified surveillance of other individuals. Unbeknownst to the Government, this production did not include 41 intercepted telephone calls involving Saipov (the "Additional Saipov Intercepts") collected in the course of those investigations. Following an inquiry from the defense in April 2020, the Additional Saipov Intercepts were identified and subsequently produced on July 15 and 24, 2020, along with five additional calls. FN 1

The Government should have identified and produced the Additional Saipov Intercepts earlier, and we do not seek to excuse their late production through this letter. The Government explains below how the Additional Saipov Intercepts were identified, as well as the additional diligence the Government has undertaken since then to ensure its compliance with Rule 16. The Government further describes additional discovery diligence conducted since April 2020 in the Classified Supplement.

FN 1 These five additional calls (dated August 16, 2015, September 9, 2015, October 2, 2015, March 21, 2016, and June 13, 2016) were subject to the protective order entered by the Court on October 29, 2019 (Dkt. No. 191 at 2-3), and are addressed further in an ex parte classified supplement to this letter (the "Classified Supplement"). The Government discovered today that it produced these five calls on July 24, 2020 though the calls are subject to the protective order. The Classified Supplement addresses topics raised in the Government's motion pursuant to Section 4 of the Classified Information Procedures Act ("CIPA"). Thus, the Government respectfully submits that the Court should review the Classified Supplement in camera and ex parte because it addresses matters subject to the protective order entered by the Court on October 29, 2019.

The Government's late production of the Additional Saipov Intercepts was the result of inadvertent human and technical errors. The undersigned prosecutors have worked in good faith for years to comply with their discovery obligations, respond to discovery requests and questions from the defense, and provide documents and information well beyond what Rule 16 requires.

Given that context, the defendant's suggestions of intentional or outrageous misconduct are unfounded and thus no evidentiary hearing is required.

If the defense believes that the Additional Saipov Intercepts provide a basis for reconsidering the discovery motion, reopening the suppression hearing, and/or seeking other relief, the defense should file an appropriate motion or motions setting forth the bases for those requests. See, e.g., United States v. Blumenberg, 506 F. App'x 53, 54 (2d Cir. 2012) ("[R]econsideration will generally be denied unless the moving party can point to controlling decisions or data that the court overlooked—matters, in other words, that might reasonably be expected to alter the conclusion reached by the court." (citation and internal quotation marks omitted)); United States v. Tzakis, 736 F.2d 867, 872 (2d Cir. 1984) (denying motion to reopen suppression hearing because of defendant's failure to develop "any significant, new factual matters that would have been developed at such a hearing"); United States v. Oliver, 626 F.2d 254, 260 (2d Cir. 1980) (same).

The Government does not object to Saipov filing such submissions, but they should not be *ex parte* and the Government should have an opportunity to respond to them. The Government ultimately believes that any such motions would be without merit. Like the interceptions produced in November 2018, the Additional Saipov Intercepts captured innocuous and non-pertinent conversations about topics including Saipov's work, family, friends, and travel."

....Now on November 25, 2020 the US has told Judge Broderick Saipov can have two video calls with family in December, if he foregoes legal VTCs: "Re: United States v. Sayfullo Habibullaevic Saipov, S1 17 Cr. 722 (VSB)

Dear Judge Broderick: We write on behalf of the parties in response to the Court's October 27, 2020 order regarding social video teleconferences ("VTCs"). The defendant requests that the Court again direct the Metropolitan Correctional Center ("MCC") to provide the defendant with two 30-minute VTCs with his SAMs-approved family members in the month of December. The Government understands that the MCC has not yet resumed in-person visits and the availability of VTCs remains the same.

Accordingly, the Government has no objection to the defendant's request on the condition that the defendant, as he has done in the past, foregoes his legal VTCs to accommodate his social VTCs. The parties also respectfully request the opportunity to update the Court about this issue on or before December 28, 2020. Respectfully submitted, AUDREY STRAUSS Acting United States Attorney By: /s/ Amanda Houle / Sidhardha Kamaraju Matthew Laroche / Jason A. Richman."

...On May 17, 2021, Judge Broderick has said he wants to hear more about Saipov's request for delay: "ORDER as to Sayfullo Habibullaevic Saipov: I am in receipt of Defendant Saipovs May 13, 2021 letter motion asserting that it is premature to schedule Rule 15 depositions and a tentative trial date given the current risk of traveling to Uzbekistan. (Doc. 379.) I would like to discuss these issues with the parties. Therefore, a telephone conference is scheduled in this matter for June 3, 2021."

On June 3, 2021 U.S. District Court for the Southern District of New York Judge Vernon S. Broderick held a conference on the case and Inner City Press live tweeted it, here and below.

The upshot? Federal Defenders do not want to travel to Uzbekistan despite a State Department authorization. And they want to wait to see if new Attorney General Garland issues a policy against seeking the death penalty. It is strongly implied that Saipov would plead guilty to life without parole. Judge Broderick wants to move things along. Podcast here.

The June 3, 2021 thread:

The Assistant US Attorney says the US State Dep't has approved discovery trip to Uzbekistan including "no quarantine when back."

Judge Broderick asks, Even if it's mission critical, aren't the health risks the same?

AUSA: Things seem to be getting better.

Judge Broderick: What if the alert is still in place in June when the parties might sit for the Rule 15 deposition?

AUSA: If things change, we'll adjust. Sure, it's Level 4. But the State Department has approved it.

Judge Broderick: Have the Federal Defenders ever before gone to a "Do Not Travel" location?

AUSA: Yes, there's an EDNY case...

AUSA: People in Uzbekistan are paying enough attention to our courthouse that they write to us and say, We see that you have big courtrooms ready for trials. So we want to move on this.

Federal Defender: I am not going to send people there, with other international organizations saying Don't go there, even if you're vaccinated. So I don't think it makes sense to schedule aspirational dates, it would impact the court generally.

Federal Defender: We also have a different Administration, which will be reviewing all capital cases. We would like time to consider applying for de-authorization.

[It had been the Orange Man who had publicly called for Saipov to be executed, soon after the massacre. Would Joe Biden and his AG Merrick Garland de-authorize the use of the death penalty here? If not, why not?]

Judge Broderick: Is there any reason the parties can't now complete the discussion of the protocols taking into account both COVID and the travel danger issues?

AUSA: Yes, those discussions should be had. And, we will do the Rule 15 somewhere outside of Uzbekistan, perhaps Kazakhstan.

Judge Broderick: At some point you just have to make a decision. How much difference is there going to be, between Uzbekistan and Kazakhstan? It seems that the defense doesn't want to do it under the requirements that the government of Uzbekistan may have. Let me hear from the government, then I'll address the deauthorization issue.

AUSA: We was not aware there were still these issues. We didn't know that Federal Defenders had issues with Kazakhstan, too. It's disconcerting. We were almost ready, back in March [2020]. Mr. Patton, from his public and non-public sources, probably knows more than I do about the DOJ de-authorization process.

AUSA: There have been some applications made to the DOJ. There is a protocol in place for it to happen. And, we submit, it should happen now.

FD Patton: On logistics, we talked about this last year. I can point to the transcript. And we talked about it off the record as well. The US Attorney's Office declined to talk with us about it and said, Let's take it to the judge. We want to petition for de-authorization, but we're waiting to see if there is a policy change coming.

Patton: If the government is willing to resolve this case with an offer of life without parole, we would like to go down that path.

Judge Broderick: Policy changes can take some time. Do you know when it's going to happen? There is a process in place for de-authorization. You could apply in this case. What is your time frame?

FD Patton: I don't know when DOJ will issue new guidance. It came up in Attorney General Garland's confirmation process. But I don't know when... Let me put a finer point on it. If the death penalty were off the table, I don't think there would be a questionnaire. I don't think there would be a trial.

AUSA: We can't wait for a policy change. What if it comes and then Mr. Patton says he's hearing rumors that might change?

Judge Broderick: On the de-authorization issue, I need to hear more. My inclination is to tell you, Mr. Patton, to move forward with applying... Is the DOJ machinery, in this

Administration, up and running? Can they decide on [de-authorization] applications submitted? I'd like the defense to explain what prejudice it would suffer by applying. 2 weeks, meet & confer. I'll exclude the time to 30 days from now under the Speedy Trial Act. Anything else?

AUSA: Our June 9 letter is obviated by the new deadline?

Judge Broderick: Yes.

It was strange, looking back, to see that the whole trial and death penalty phase could have been avoided if, once Joe Biden was elected and Merrick Garland confirmed, execution had been taken off the table. Why wasn't it?

...On June 14, 2021, from TheHill.com: DOJ asked the Supreme Court to revive the "Boston Marathon bomber's" death sentence. DOJ asked the justices to reverse a Boston-based federal appeals court that vacated the death sentence for Dzhokhar Tsarnaev, the lone surviving perpetrator of the 2013 attack.

"[T]he jury carefully considered each of respondent's crimes and determined that capital punishment was warranted for the horrors that he personally inflicted — setting down a shrapnel bomb in a crowd and detonating it, killing a child and a promising young student, and consigning several others to a lifetime of unimaginable suffering," the DOJ's brief reads. "That determination by 12 conscientious jurors deserves respect and reinstatement by this Court." Brief here.

Now on June 22, Judge Broderick has requested a status report on Saipov's lawyers' de-authorization request in 45 days: "The parties are directed to file a status update on the de-authorization request and a progress report on the negotiation of the Rule 15 deposition protocols within 45 days. (Signed by Judge Vernon S. Broderick on 6/21/21)."

...On August 6 the US wrote to Judge Broderick that depositions in Uzbekistan in the Fall of 2021 would be fine. But Saipov's Federal Defenders said not so fast, the government there wants to sit in and anyway, new SDNY COVID policy amid the Delta variant will not allow enough jurors. They note that "over 50 countries are currently at Level 4 of the State Department's travel advisory, including the UK, Ireland, Greece, the Kyrgyz Republic, Portugal, Cuba, South Africa, the BVI, the Maldives and the Netherlands."

And yet the UN still planned an "honor system" no-vax General Assembly week on September 21, 2021. Kurt would cover it from the UN Gate.

...On August 12, 2021 Judge Broderick has sided with the defense:

"ENDORSEMENT: Given the low vaccination rate in Uzbekistan and the rising COVID-19 infection rate, I find that it is premature to schedule Rule 15 depositions at this time. Within 30 days, the parties should file a joint status letter updating me on their discussions regarding alternate locations for the depositions and the protocol that will be used. The parties should inform me whether any of the countries proposed by defense counsel are viable options. The parties are also directed to update me within 30 days regarding defendant's potential deauthorization request."

On September 10, 2021, the eve of 9/11, the US Attorney's Office has filed a letter saying it is reviewing unnamed countries for "travel conditions in light of the pandemic."

On September 27, 2021, weeks after the US Attorney's Office filed a letter saying it was reviewing unnamed countries for "travel conditions in light of the pandemic," Judge Broderick held another proceeding. Inner City Press again covered it.

The US said it just heard that a "neighboring country" would allow depositions without the ground rules the defense had questioned. But the defense still have questions, and Judge Broderick said since he has a civil trial from June 27 to approximately July 15, 2022, this trial might well be after that.

And it was...

Letters were filed on October 8, 2021. The US wants the trial in the second quarter of 2022, pointing out among other things that prosecutors in a Somali piracy prosecution in the EDNY recently went and conducted depositions in that country. US v. Mohammed, 18-cr-603 (ARR).

The Federal Defenders want the fourth quarter of 2022, contrasting the jury selection issues with those of Ghislaine Maxwell - Jeffrey Epstein's recruiter and trafficker, see "Maximum Maxwell" https://www.amazon.com/gp/product/B09PFR6M8N/

Federal Defenders also say that Learned Counsel David Stern has a trial starting February 9, 2022 in EDNY, US v. Kandic, 17-cr-449 (NGG). Now it's up to Judge Broderick - and the Committee, and virus.

On November 29, 2021 Judge Broderick picked:

"ORDER as to Sayfullo Habibullaevic Saipov. On November 29, 2021, I held a conference in this case. In accordance with my comments made during the conference, by or before December 6, 2021, the parties are directed to meet and confer and to jointly propose a trial schedule for a trial beginning August 15, 2022. For the reasons stated on the record, the speedy trial time is excluded through August 15, 2022, in the interests of justice under the Speedy Trial Act pursuant to 18 U.S.C. § 3161(h)(7)(A). SO ORDERED. (Signed by Judge Vernon S. Broderick on 11/29/21)"

On May 4, 2022 U.S. District Court for the Southern District of New York Judge Vernon S. Broderick held a conference on the case and Inner City Press live tweeted it here and below.

Along with discussion of jury selection procedures and a pending request by Federal Defenders to deauthorize the use of the death penalty, the burning issue of Saipov's desire for a battery for his clock radio, or a hand cranked radio arose.

Also, that he (or his lawyers) want only vaccinated jurors. The thread:

OK- now case of West Side Highway van terror driver Saipov, in person in 23B. Judge Broderick rushes in with a suit bag, presumably containing his judicial robes.

Judge Broderick wants a pool of 1000 jurors in August. It seems there is a potential for strong feelings (even) higher than in current Hezbollah trial of Alexei Saab (that jury was still deliberating - they found him guilty)

Judge Broderick increases his estimate of length of Saipov trial to 3 months. The US says from August jury selection, Tell them to be available into January, citing "penalty phase."

Federal Defenders says they want to present video testimony from overseas.

Kurt noted: This case has a big public budget. Why didn't Federal Defenders represent Alexei Saab?

Judge Broderick muses that the Ghislaine Maxwell trial took off between Chistmas and New Year. Actually, no: after days off for 2d Circuit confirmation, jury continued past Chistmas to Dec 29. Maximum Maxwell

 The question arose: How to not let jurors see Saipov's leg chains? Judge Broderick says to use cloth, so no one's feet are visible.

 Federal Defender Patton says he filed deauthorization (of death penalty for Saipov) request filed with DOJ on Feb 23, 2022. No ruling yet.

FD Patton says he wants a vaccination requirement on Saipov jurors.

Judge Broderick: Even people who are vaccinated contract the virus.

Federal Defender Andrew Dalack (standby counsel for Michael Avenatti, also ultimately convicted) says in the MDC jail Saipov can't get batteries for his radio alarm clock, for prayers. Dalack may ask Judge Broderick to order a hand-crank radio. Ramadan provisions are now moot.

On July 18, 2022 Judge Broderick ordered:

"ORDER as to Sayfullo Habibullaevic Saipov: I am in receipt of several requests to amend the pretrial schedule. Since potential jurors will now complete questionnaires over the course of August 11, 12, 17, 18, and 19, 2022, the parties competing proposals to revise the jury selection schedule are both DENIED. (Doc. 451.)

As previously indicated by my order of July 14, 2022, the joint request to revise the *in limine* motion schedule is GRANTED. (Doc. 456, 458.) The parties shall hereby comply with the following pretrial schedule for both the guilt and, if necessary, penalty phases:

Updated Motions in Limine: August 5, 2022 Motions in limine due. August 19, 2022 Responses to motions in limine due. September 2, 2022 Replies to motions in limine due. September 19, 2022 Argument, if necessary, on motions in limine."

On August 3, 2022, this: "On July 29, 2022, I ordered that the parties appear for a conference on August 10, 2022, at 4:00 p.m., and advised that the Court would provide courtroom location information by separate order. (Doc. 461.) It is hereby ORDERED that the conference will take place in Courtroom 318 at 40 Foley Square, New York, NY 10007. There will be no dial-in."

Kurt asked: Why not? Why no dial-in? Why take this death penalty trial dark, limited to only those who can enter the courtroom (when the Judge would later order the press out of the courtroom, subsequently reversed?) In DDC, they had expected the CARES Act and its call-in lines through at least November. Is there not more COVID in NYC than DC? Did this act not impact many in the public?

On August 15, 2022, Saipov's non Federal Defender counsel wrote in with more urging for only vaccinated jurors, detailing how

Eastern District of New York Judge Nicholas G. Garaufis did this in *US v. Kandic*, in April 2022: "if unvaccinated questioning briefly continued and the prospective juror was then excused. This was primarily done to avoid the risk of discussion between jurors... for fear other jurors migth seize on it as a convenient excuse to avoid jury duty. The parties did not require proof of the jurors' vaccination." We'll have more on this.

On August 16, 2022 Judge Broderick asked for more information:

"on or before August 24, 2022, the Defense indicate whether it intends to request Mr. Saipov be permitted to take breaks to pray during jury selection and trial, and, if so, to provide the daily prayer schedule Mr. Saipov intends to adhere to for the months of October, November, and December 2022, and January 2023. The Government's response should address whether any members of the Government team are unvaccinated."

On August 23, 2022 Judge Broderick docketed his disclosure to the parties:

"ORDER as to Sayfullo Habibullaevic Saipov. On August 20, 2022, potential juror #943 left a voicemail with my Chambers. I have notified the parties of this voicemail, and provided a copy to them. Accordingly, it is hereby ORDERED that the parties can take the voicemail into consideration when evaluating potential juror #943 for service. SO ORDERED. (Signed by Judge Vernon S. Broderick on 8/23/22)."

If in cases like US v. Ghislaine Maxwell juror questionnaire information was made public, why not this voicemail, so the public can understand?

On August 25, 2022 the Federal Defenders alleged massive Brady disclosure violations by DOJ, including evidence "that he was influenced by others who share culpability yet they are not being prosecuted, much less facing the death penalty." They want a hearing.

On August 29, 2022 the Federal Defenders wrote in again, now demanding that the October 11 trial be postponed. They say the new document show or go to that Saipov "was radicalized or perhaps even groomed by a network of Uzbek extremists."

On September 12, 2022 Judge Broderick granted the request for vaxed-only jurors, and more:

"ORDER as to Sayfullo Habibullaevic Saipov... Accordingly, it is hereby ORDERED that an individual may not be seated as a juror in the above-captioned case unless at least two weeks have passed since the individual's second dose in a two-dose series, such as the Pfizer-BioNTech and Moderna vaccines, or at least two weeks have passed since the individual's single-dose J&J/Janssen vaccine.

IT IS FURTHER ORDERED that, notwithstanding any courthouse policies to the contrary, all individuals in the courtroom during the trial in the above-captioned case must wear masks, except for witnesses while testifying and counsel when questioning from the podium. IT IS FURTHER ORDERED that, notwithstanding any courthouse policies to the contrary, jurors must wear masks in the jury room unless eating or drinking, in which case, jurors are directed to remain at least six feet apart. IT IS FURTHER ORDERED that everyone must otherwise abide by all COVID protocols in place for the courthouse. SO ORDERED. (Signed by Judge Vernon S. Broderick on 9/12/22)."

On September 16, 2022 this from the prosecutors: "Re: United States v. Sayfullo Habibullaevic Saipov, S1 17 Cr. 722 (VSB)

Dear Judge Broderick: The Court has previously requested updates on the status of the defendant's request to the Attorney General to withdraw the Notice of Intent to Seek the Death Penalty in this case. (Dkt. No. 80). We were notified today that the Attorney General has decided to continue to seek the death penalty. We conveyed this decision to defense counsel and the victims." Letter on Inner City Press' DocumentCloud here.

This came days before the UN General Assembly week, on a day US Ambassador to the UN Linda Thomas-Greenfield said the

Biden administration is all about promoting UN principles. But those include no death penalty. And USUN has done nothing to stop the UN from banning the Press.

And docketed October, 2022: "ORDER as to Sayfullo Habibullaevic Saipov: ORDERED that the Bureau of Prisons (Metropolitan Detention Center, Brooklyn) and the United States Marshals Service accept the following clothing for Mr. Saipov, Register Number 79715-054, and permit him to wear it for appearances at trial: 1. Four shirts; 2. two pairs of pants; 3. two ties; 4. one belt; 5. one suit jacket; 6. one pair of shoes; 7. four pairs of dress socks; 8. four undershirts; and 9. one sweater. (Signed by Judge Vernon S. Broderick on 9/30/2022)."

And on October 5, 2022 this: "ORDER as to Sayfullo Habibullaevic Saipov. Given that the Defense intends to submit an additional reply in support of its Brady motion by October 5, 2022, (Doc. 587), I do not intend to make a ruling on the Defense's Brady motion during the Final Pretrial Conference. The parties also asked in their email whether the list of jurors scheduled to appear on the first two days of jury selection is finalized and, if so, whether the parties can be provided a copy of the list.

The Jury Department has finalized the list of jurors, with the prospective jurors to be stricken for cause redacted ("Redacted List of Jurors"). A copy of the Redacted List of Jurors will be sent to the parties by email and filed under seal. At the start of individual voir dire, we will summon 15 jurors a day, in order of juror number, and will continue that process until we have qualified a sufficient number of prospective jurors. As jury selection progresses, I will revisit whether to summon more or fewer jurors each day (Signed by Judge Vernon S. Broderick on 10/5/22)."

On Columbus Day, October 10, 2022 - the day before jury selection - Saipov's Federal Defenders filed a motion to stay the proceedings, based on racial disparities in the jury pool, including the exclusion of "inactive" voters. Would Judge Broderick grant it?

On October 13, 2022 Saipov's Federal Defenders wrote to object to any disqualification of anti-death penalty jurors, focusing on Juror 17 who cited his religious opposition to the death penalty. They argue that exclusion would violate the Free Exercise Clause of the First Amendment.

Kurt noted: But inclusion would guarantee no death penalty imposed.

On October 21, 2022 Judge Broderick asked for filings on whether Saipov can waive his attendance at his own death penalty trial, and if he could be compelled to attend, or to watch it on a screen:

"ORDER as to Sayfullo Habibullaevic Saipov. It is hereby ORDERED that the defense submit a supplemental letter motion by November 4, 2022, in support of the position that Mr. Saipov, as a defendant in a capital case, can waive his appearance at all stages of trial. IT IS FURTHER ORDERED that the Government submit a letter by November 11, 2022, stating its position concerning whether Mr. Saipov, as a defendant in a capital case, can waive his appearance at trial after jury selection. IT IS FURTHER ORDERED that the Governments November 11 letter also state its views, if any, concerning the questions posed above to the defense, including whether I can compel Mr. Saipov's attendance at trial, and the legality and/or propriety of arranging for Mr. Saipov to electronically watch the trial should I grant his waiver (Signed by Judge Vernon S. Broderick on 10/21/22)."

On November 2, 2022, jury selection continued. Judge Broderick sat in the jury box, and a prospective juror said to be from the Paul Weiss law firm was in the Plexiglass witness box.

With the prospective juror out of the room, Judge Broderick said he'll ask for the law firm's human resources policy, which he assumes will be in writing, but will not strike the juror for cause.

Upon her return, she asked if jurors will be able to take notes during the trial. Yes but not to share them, Judge Broderick replies.

On November 3, 2022 Judge Broderick docketed an order about speeding up the process:

   "ORDER as to Sayfullo Habibullaevic Saipov: Accordingly, beginning the week of November 7, 2022, I intend to limit follow-up questions to only those necessary to clarify any genuine ambiguity as to whether a prospective juror is qualified to serve on this capital jury. In other words, if I determine that additional inquiry is necessary to determine whether the juror is qualified, I will ask appropriate follow-up questions, but as a general matter, I will no longer ask follow-up questions proposed by the parties.

Further, I assume that the parties' proposed personalized voir dire questions to date have included all of the questions necessary in light of a prospective jurors answers to the questionnaire. If either party believes that I do not have the legal authority to take the actions outlined in this order or that taking such actions would be otherwise legally objectionable, that party shall file a letter on or before November 4, 2022. (Signed by Judge Vernon S. Broderick on 11/2/2022)."

On November 8, 2022 with the SDNY courthouse largely closed for Election Day, Saipov's Federal Defenders filed a 94-page omnibus challenge to the US' penalty phase presentation, with many redactions. It seeks to "exclude or limit evidence of his alleged terrorist-support motive" and his lack of remorse.

A sample redaction: "The Court should exclude or limit evidence of [REDACTED] as evidence that Mr. Saipov will commit acts of violence in solitary confinement in the SAMs Unit at ADX Florence," later described as H-unit, where Thomas Silverstein (d. 2019) and Ramzi Yousef have been housed."

As to Silverstein, later an artist, note despite the allegations of being held incommunicado this website: https://thomassilverstein.net/

On November 10, 2022 Judge Broderick to his credit ordered Saipov's Federal Defenders to provide written justification for the redactions:

"Application denied without prejudice to renewal. There is a presumption of public access to anything that qualifies as a "judicial document," i.e., a "filed item that is 'relevant to the performance of the judicial function and useful in the judicial process.'" Bernstein v. Bernstein Litowitz Berger & Grossmann LLP, 814 F.3d 132, 139 (2d Cir. 2016) (quoting Lugosch v. Pyramid Co. of Onondaga, 435 F.3d 110, 119 (2d Cir. 2006)). The presumption is "at its strongest" when "the information at issue forms the basis of the court's adjudication." Liberty Re (Bermuda) Ltd. v. Transamerica Occidental Life Ins. Co., No. 04 Civ. 5044(NRB), 2005 WL 1216292, at *6 (S.D.N.Y. May 23, 2005) (citation omitted).

Accordingly, on or before November 17, 2022, the Defense shall file a letter motion demonstrating, with legal authority, countervailing factors justifying the Defense's proposed redactions to its omnibus challenge and to my Opinion & Order of October 7, 2022, and how those countervailing factors overcome the presumption in favor of public access to judicial documents."

On November 16, 2022 Judge Broderick was again in the jury box, and the process continued. Inner City Press was alone in the gallery and noted as

"Prospective juror 371 is struck for hardship, she would only be paid $40 a day for 3 days.

"Now the US wants juror 360 out, could only order execution for Osama bin Laden, Newtown or Parkland mass shootings, for anyone else there'd be a 'high bar.' Federal Defenders not surprisingly say this juror would be OK.

Judge Broderick says answers were ambiguous, juror will be excused. FD wants to ask more questions.

There followed arguments about what questions to ask.

* * *

On November 21, 2022 there came Juror 380, a research lab scientist "generally opposed to the death penalty" who had Googled the case after his first encounter at SDNY with it. Inner City Press thread:

OK -now at death penalty jury selection in US v Saipov. Juror 380 runs a research lab at [a hospital], wants out. Says he understands the trial is to start "next year."

Juror 380: I have three university conferences in early 2023.

Judge Broderick: Do you have documentation of that? In December, January and February. Since you filled out the questionnaire in August, have you seen anything about Mr Saipov?

Juror 380: On a website. I Googled.

Judge: Could you avoid that in the future?

Juror 380: Yes.

Judge: Are you fully vaccinated?

Juror 380: Yes.

Judge: You said a friend of yours is a public defender in this courthouse. How often do you speak with him?

Juror 380: Once a year.

... On November 28, 2022 prospective juror 435, a 22-year-old woman with short hair in a black and white floral print shirt, was in the witness box. She first said she could not envision imposing the death penalty - then said that if the majority voted for it, she would go along.

(*Sheep*, someone said).

She was asked to step out, and the AUSA moved to strike. The head Federal Defender said he did not oppose.

Judge Broderick said this might be the first time both sides would have moved to strike. When the Juror, now non-juror, 435 came back in, Judge Broderick said she was excused, and could now tell her parents what the case is about, if she chooses. The process proceeds.

On November 30, prospective juror 162 was called back to ask about her hardship, who would pick up her son if she served on the jury. With the juror out of the room, Judge Broderick said he would excuse her, not wanting to cause the couple to for the first time use a non-family member for child care, at their expense.

In the course of this, Judge Broderick said selected jurors might be called back in on December 19 or 20 - and the opening arguments will be on January 3, in a two or three month trial.

On December 5, that January 3 date was repeated, with Juror 44, thread here:

Juror 44 says he'd be paid during trial, his concern is if he'd still have his job after 3 months.

Judge Broderick again says it will start on January 3, 2023.

Juror 44 says he's watched "morbid, Dateline-like shows" about life in prison. He mentions Folsom and other prisons in California. And subjugation of women.

Judge: Can you put that out of your mind?

Juror 44: Yes. But given what's happening in Iran...

Juror 44 says he favors the death penalty, where no remorse "like the BTK killer, or Charles Manson." He himself spent one night in jail (and got an order of protection against him).

Juror 44: Death penalty is to punish evil crimes, those with no remorse. But living in prison could be worse.

On December 6, juror 465 was in the box. When asked if he could consider Saipov's childhood as possibly militating for life in prison instead of execution, If it comes to that, he said Yes.

But both sides agreed, with him out of the room, that his previous answers had been unclear. He was excused.

Jump cut to December 12, 2022. Inner City Press went up to the 24th floor courtroom and found inside two prosecutors, and Judge Broderick shown on TV monitors.

Later into the docket, Federal Defenders wrote, "the parties have considered the virtual alternative that the Court proposed earlier today, specifically, proceeding with voir dire via Microsoft Teams for the next few days, between now and when Your Honor is allowed to return to the courthouse pursuant to the SDNY COVID protocols. The defense does not object."

On December 20, 2022 Saipov's Federal Defenders objected to the US Attorney's Office using 14 of its 20 peremptory strikes... against women.

On December 22, the US struck back, pointing out that Team Saipov used 12 of its 20 peremptories against women, "the defendant's Batson challenge may be rejected on that ground alone." But of course, there's more.

On Friday, December 23, Judge Broderick continued jury selection. Inner City Press live-tweeted, thread here:

OK- Now again in US v Saipov death penalty eligible case jury selection, Dec 23 past 4 pm. Judge Broderick says trial will start Jan 9, and run to end of March.

Juror 707 has a ticket to Jamaica March 23, is heading down to e-mail it to the Court.

Juror 707 has returned and is being excused, as is Juror 713 who answered "N/A" on the questionnaire when asked for views on the death penalty.

It's past 5 pm, with jurors 714 and 720 still to be questioned, 723, 724 and 732 to be told to return another day. Questionnaire was in August, then for a January 3 trial. Now with jury selection still not over, the trial is pushed to January 9.

Juror 714 has said that as a Catholic she is against the death penalty, favors life imprisonment, and would only vote for that. She will be questioned 20 or 25 more minutes; 720 is being sent home after waiting for a long time.

Juror 714: I would not want to carry the burden of having voted to impose the death penalty.

Federal Defenders still want her, it seems. But juror 714 is struck for cause. And juror 720 cried before she left. Adjourned.

Meanwhile, the Federal Defenders filed a letter complaining about the halal meals in the MDC jail - just peanut butter and jelly - and asking for Federal Defenders to feed Saipov lunch during the trial.

On January 3, 2023, while the Federal Defenders' motion for a prayer rug protocol was approved, individual *voir dire* continued, and Inner City Press was there, the only media in the courtroom:

OK- Now again in jury selection, Jan 3. Juror 764 says the Middle East is just "tribes." US wanted more questions, but juror is qualified. Is told not to Google "mitigating factors."

Questioning began of Juror 664 but will continue; there will be rulings on Jurors 360, 224 and 380 (in writing) and 648, orally.

On January 4, 2023 questioning of juror 780 was put over to January 5, when lead defense counsel will not be present. Judge Broderick, citing the need for US Marshals to search through food, denied the Federal Defenders' halal lunch motion. But there will apparently be an ex parte / sealed letter on the topic.

Judge Broderick said an order would issue that night or the next day about the overflow courtroom and logistics. He questioned whether the statute is about victims being in the courtroom itself, and not any overflow room. A concern was expressed about victims sitting in what was referred to as the press box.

[Later, Judge Broderick would try to give the Press spots to others - and it would be opposed.]

On January 6, 2023 after a long jury selection that Inner City Press covered, some below, Judge Broderick confirmed that the trial starts January 9, with masks:

"as to Sayfullo Habibullaevic Saipov: As voir dire has concluded, it is hereby ORDERED that the trial shall begin on Monday, January 9, 2023... Any victims and victim's family members in attendance will be given priority seating in Courtroom 24B. See 18 U.S.C. § 3510. it is hereby ordered that all people present in Courtroom 24B are required to wear a face mask, except for witnesses while testifying and counsel when questioning from the podium."

And so it began...

On January 9, 2023, Inner City Press was presented and live-tweeted, thread here:

OK - Death penalty trial of Sayfullo Saipov for killing 8 on NYC's West Side Highway bike path is starting.

In the courtroom, the prosecutors are at the front table, ready. Saipov's lawyers are standing with the chair in the middle of their table empty, waiting for Saipov. Down in the courthouse lobby, an entourage awaited the arrival of FBI bigwigs for opening statements.

Saipov's Federal Defenders have filed motions and even a sealed / ex parte letter about themselves bringing him halal lunch during trial, and where to store his prayer rug. But where is Saipov? Even the empty seat at the defense table seems set for a lawyer.

All rise!

Judge Vernon S. Broderick: Mr. Saipov, can you understand the interpreter?

Saipov: Yes!

Judge: I received counsel's e-mail about questioning jurors 185 and 660. I will do that. But Juror 37 first, on any assistance for her to hear the proceedings.

Note: Jury selection went on for weeks - months - but was still not finished. FBI bigshots and victims arrive for opening arguments, and there are still questions for three jurors, to be whispered at sidebar. When will the transcript be available? At what cost?

Update: One lawyer for each side went forward (Federal Defenders' David Patton and Assistant US Attorney Amanda Houle). Saipov is setting at defense table in a white COVID mask, with four defense lawyers in black masks.

Judge Broderick is back and says: Let's go back on the record. About GX 1145, does the Government intend to only show 1145T, the translation?

AUSA Houle: We would just reference the videos.

Judge: If your opening? AUSA: Yes.

Judge (in ruling voice): Defense claims prejudice.

Judge: The defense claims that showing the van hitting the school bus is prejudicial. Ms. Houle, how much would you describe?

AUSA Houle: Generally describe the occupants of the school bus.

Judge: I have watched the exhibit several times. I will allow reference

Judge Broderick: But I exclude the comments of the person taking the video. With regard to GX404, is there a witness who will testify about it?

AUSA: Yes.

Judge: The person who took the video?

AUSA: No, Your Honor. Someone who was inside the bus will be testifying.

Judge: Will you blur the children's faces ? I only thought of this last night...

AUSA: We'll confer with the defense. We've spoken with the family of the child in GX410, and will do so again.

Federal Defender Patton: Please tell the jurors to not use the cafeteria.

Judge: OK. Ms. Rodriguez, please bring the jury out.

[During the long wait, Saipov is playing with / working on his interpretation headphones. Jury enters and is sworn.]

Judge Broderick: Jurors, you are the triers of fact. Mr. Saipov is accused of intentionally killing eight people, and injuring 18 others. For these, 26 counts. Then, attempt to join ISIS, and killing while destroying the truck. He has pleaded not guilty. You must presume he is innocent.

Judge: Jurors, about the trial, you may not tweet or blog or discuss - even with yourselves. Now, the openings.

AUSA Alexander Li: On the West Side there is a bike path. On Oct 31, 2017, it was the scene of horror. There was a bus, with children. It was done by Saipov.

AUSA Li: He crushed their bodies, left them bleeding to die. He ended eight lives in his vicious attack. Why? He proudly said he did it for ISIS, the brutal terrorist organization. He killed to become a member of ISIS, right here in New York.

AUSA Li: He joined ISIS in 2014, using an encrypted app. There was a photo of a bloody tire, with the caption, Run over them without mercy. He started planning. He planned to mow down people from the West Side to the Brooklyn Bridge. He rented a Home Depot truck.

AUSA Li: He drove the pickup truck into Manhattan. At Pier 40, he struck. He raced onto the bike path. He plowed through a family that was visiting from Belgium. He murdered a woman. Then he hit a second family from Belgium. The wife lost her legs.

AUSA Li: He struck a group from Argentina, killing all of those on the left side. He murdered five of them. He swerved toward a woman from New Jersey. He ran over two young Americans. Then he crashed into a school bus, with two children in it.

AUSA Li: He had knives and fake guns. He jumped out yelling, Allahu akbar! He aimed the guns at police, who shot him. The attack was over. At the hospital, he spoke to the FBI, proudly. He wanted to display an ISIS flag in his hospital room.

AUSA Li: We will show the knives, and his notes. You will hear from witness about the roar of the engine, the searing pain... We'll show you video of him in Home Depot, and video of the school bus. The racketeering conspiracy in the indictment is ISIS.

AUSA Li: We ask that you follow Judge Broderick's instructions on the law and use common sense. If you do, you will find the defendant guilty.

Judge Broderick: We'll take our lunch break now.

* * * *

On January 10, 2023, witnesses from families run over by Saipov testified, with interpreters, and the day ended with a video of Home Depot. One juror wanted to ask questions about Saipov' driver's license, another if he is an alternate. Inner City Press was there, thread here:

OK - now Day 2: jury called in more than an hour late (they had questions).

The day's first witness is Joanna Maroudas, FBI Special Agent for 19 years. She did the post-arrest interview of Saipov.

Maroudas: He is wearing a green top, at back table.

AUSA: Did he tell you what he had done?

Maroudas: He rented a truck to kill people. He said Abu Bakr al Baghdadi told him to conduct the attack. He's the former leader of ISIS.

AUSA: Where did the interview take place?

Maroudas: In Bellevue Hospital. He asked to hang the ISIS flag. He smiled.

Now cross-examination of FBI's Maroudas by Federal Defender Sylvie Levine.

FD Levine: Mr. Saipov gave you consent to search his phones?

Maroudas: Yes. I started going through it right then.

FD Levine: He answered all of your questions?

Maroudas: Most of them. Not all.

 The next witness is from the tourist group, with an interpreter, testifying that along with visiting Top of the Rock(efeller Center) and, ironically, the site of 9/11/01, rented bikes from Blazing Saddles and biked down perimeter of Manhattan, 9A. Judge Broderick calls the lunch break.

Saipov's Federal Defenders [wisely] decide not to cross examine the first victim-family witness. Next US witness is also from Belgium.

She says: I traveled to New York with my mom and my two sisters, on October 28. We rented bicycles from Blazing Saddles.

Witness: The truck was red and black. My sister was screaming (sobs). I turned around and saw her lying next to her bicycle. She was unconscious and there was blood coming out of her nose and mouth. I tried to remember a first aid course I took.

[Again, no cross-examination]

The Saipov trial day ends with video of Home Depot - Judge Broderick tells jurors not to Google or talk to anyone about the case. Once they leave, he asks about Juror 531 who wants to know if he is an alternate.

* * *

On Day 3, there were more victims, including from Argentina - and now a five-day break, as the US case, or first part of the case, is moving quickly.

Martin Marro on the stand, he grew up in Argentina.

Assistant US Attorney: Were you hurt?

Marro: Yes. My head and ribs and elsewhere.

AUSA: Let's turn to October 31, 2017. What did you do?

Marro: I took the subway and met my friends. We went biking.... Ten of us came to New York from Argentina to celebrate. But five of us never came home. [Names them]

Witness authenticates Gov't Exhibit 225, showing twisted bicycle carnage and the West Side Highway.

Next witness is Mr. Zhang, who started working at Stuyvesant High School in 2015.

Assistant US Attorney: Were you working on the afternoon of Oct ober31, 2017?

Zhang: Yes. I was looking for the CitiBike station after work.

AUSA: Did you take one?

Zhang: I was going to ride home on the bike path. I saw the truck, going very fast... I saw a body, that was not moving. I did not go closer. I was about 15 yards away.

Next witness is FBI Crisis Management Squad member Jessica Huckemeyer. The AUSA lays groundwork, then reads a Government Exhibit, stipulation about deceased victims and evidence. GX 3 identifies where law enforcement found the decedents..

* * *

On January 16, 2023 - MLK Day - the Federal Defenders filed a motion or notice with Judge Broderick that if Saipov is convicted in this liability stage of any capital count, the alternate jurors should be dismissed, under the Federal Death Penalty Act. This means that losing a single juror in the second phase would put it all back to square one, August 2022.

On January 17 the trial re-started... sort of. A juror had emailed Judge Broderick's chamber and there ensued five hours of entirely sealed questioning of jurors. Inner City Press' live tweeted what it could, thread here:

Judge Broderick speaking before jury comes in - about a juror note that he says he won't make public at this time.

Judge Broderick: I propose to question each juror in the jury room under oath. Mr. Patton, ask your client if he will waive his presence. Any objection that we do it in the jury room?

AUSA: No.

FD Patton: No objection.

Judge Broderick said that the email was "essentially to my chambers;" it implicated other jurors and even their health-related information. No Press at the questioning, Judge Broderick said, so that jurors will be candid.

And they're baaack - after more than five hours. Here on the 24th floor, people milled around in the hall. Now Judge Broderick has retaken bench, talking about COVID tests for jurors.

Federal Defender asks, still without the jury in the box, that audio of the school bus be silenced, appearing to say that the children inside are not victims for purpose of this case.

AUSA: We are focused on the reaction of bystanders, some of whom are children.

Judge: I am going to allow into evidence Govt Exhibit 404B, but without the audio. Is the bus driver going to be a witness?

AUSA: No. We'll have another witness.

Judge: Can I see GX 410 again, and the audio?

[It is played, including "oh sh*t, are you ok?"]

It's 4:30 pm and they are bringing the jurors out for the first time of the day.

Judge: I apologize, next time I will give advance warning of questioning, there was no particular triggering event. If you feel sick, test yourself. Or you can test in the court. Just tell us. Now we'll begin with a stipulation, including about DNA swabs on the truck.

 First (and probably only) witness of the day: FBI Forensics expert Lara Adams, in from Quantico. She says "an octillion times more likely"

Judge Broderick: We're going to break for the day and continue the testimony tomorrow. Remember, no emailing. Good evening.

* * *

On January 18, the US put on experts including from the Washington Institute for Near East Affairs, on the differences - or not - between Saipov and Las Vegas shooter Stephen Paddock. Was Saipov really trying to join ISIS? Jan 18 thread here

Judge Broderick: I'm prepared to hear from the parties about the accident reconstruction expert. But let's get the jury.

Jury entering!

Judge: You may inquire.

AUSA: Ms. Adams, was Darren Drake included as a potential contributor?

Adams: Yes. Swab 93 was a mixture.

No cross examination, now next expert witness is from the Washington Institute for Near East Policy. The government / taxpayers are paying him $400 a hour.

Now Judge Broderick says Juror 37 told his deputy clerk that he is the best man in a wedding on March 16, and has a surgery on March 22 then he's "done."

Federal Defender is cross-examining US Attorney's Office's ISIS expert.

FD Patton: You're aware Mr. Saipov committed this attack on October 31, 2017, correct?

Expert: Yes.

Patton: But you're aware that ISIS' publication about it was based on media only?

Expert: Yes.

FD Patton: And when ISIS claimed credit for the Las Vegas shooting, they just made up a name, right?

Expert: I'm not ISIS, I don't know. ISIS says he converted to Islam six months before the attack.

FD Patton: You testified in Chicago in 2021?

Expert: Yes.

FD Patton: And you'll admit that ISIS has never said, Commit a martyrdom attack to become a member of ISIS, right?

Expert: It's implicit.

FD Patton: They say the motive must be purely to please Allah, correct?

[This is FD's defense against death penalty]

Re-direct examination:

AUSA: Is it right that ISIS releases content in other languages, like Uzbek?

Expert: Yes.

AUSA: How many ISIS claims of responsibility have you reviewed, and how many have you questioned?

Expert: Thousands. And no questions except Las Vegas shooting...

Jury leaves at 5:28 pm

Judge Broderick: US, how many witnesses tomorrow, with its inclement weather?

AUSA: Six, some quite short.

Judge: Will there be a defense case?

Federal Defender Patton: If there is, it will be short.

Judge: I have a Violation of Supervised Release proceeding at 9 tomorrow. So, 10 am.

Judge Broderick: I'll be asking, can the pick-up truck be the weapon, if its maximum speed is limited? I don't want answers now. We'll get together at 10. I'll allocute Mr. Saipov. And I'll try to get my act together and get you the charge tomorrow. We'll see.

* * *

On January 19, the US did not as they'd projected rest their case. The day ended with a witness who'd been in the school bus that Saipov hit (and who sued NYC for $5 million - surprisingly, Federal Defenders did not cross-examine her). Live tweeted thread here:

OK - now in death penalty trial of US v. Saipov, arguments about US' "truck speed" expert before jurors are brought in. Federal Defenders want to *voir dire* him.

Now Saipov is brought in.

Judge Broderick: Mr. Saipov, do you intend to testify?

Saipov: No.

Judge Broderick: You can change your mind at any time, until your lawyers rest your case. Bring in the jury.

Footnote: It's possible Saipov said No, not at this time

 Jury entering!

The expert worked at the Rochester Police Department, Special Accident Investigations Unit. His name is Jon Northrup.

AUSA Li: When's the last time you test-crashed a car?

Expert: Recently.

AUSA Li: What is in this photograph?

Expert Northrup: The Home Depot truck.

AUSA Li: For this case, did you rent any Home Depot trucks?

Northrup: Yes, twice.

AUSA Li: Where did this truck enter the West Side Highway?

Northrup: Houston Street, Pier 40.

Judge Broderick declares lunch break and tells jurors he hopes they brought umbrellas. Then he tells counsel he has a full calendar tomorrow. So the charge conference will be next week.

Saipov trial day nears 5 pm with witness in Creole, Ms. Charles.

AUSA: What is the reason you are not employed?

[Note: Marierose Charles sued the City for $5 million. Will Federal Defenders be inquiring on cross examination?]

Nope - Federal Defenders have no cross-examination questions for school bus witness Ms. Charles.

Judge Broderick: It's 5:30, jurors, I'll let you go until Monday, do not blog or read social media.

Then, Judge: Mr Patton, any defense case?

Patton: If so, it won't be long.

On Monday, the US will have the medical examiner. Judge Broderick said his legal instructions will be three hours long.

* * *

On January 23, the US put on as witnesses the medical examiner and a Bureau of Prisons official who searched Saipov's cell, thread here

OK - now Saipov trial resumes. Judge Broderick speaking before jury comes in - asking for arguments on Gov't Exh 1220, the "prison journal."

Judge Broderick: At first, two pages of the prison journal were photographed, then 30 pages produced. The government wants to introduce 10 pages.

Saipov's attorneys say it should be excluded since it includes prayers...

Judge Broderick: I am not excluding, but let me hear on redactions, of the writing above the drawings.

Federal Defender: These writings are from 2021, still the government argued they are relevant - but only the portion that supports their theory.

Now the US plays for jurors a Saipov prison call, and shows the transcript. He is singing a poem, presumably to his family in Uzbekistan, including the lines

"I am Allah's warrior, I am the soldier of the Caliphate."

With the jury out of courtroom (but courtroom otherwise open), Judge Broderick jokes to Federal Defender Dalack, often seen with an "M" Michigan baseball cap, that he hopes Dalack's pro sports team does better than his alma mater, in maize and blue. Defense case may be January 24.

Next US witness is a Bureau of Prisons' intelligence analyst. He searched Saipov's cell.

AUSA: Did he have his own cell?

BOP witness: Yes. In MDC Brooklyn.

He described what he found (coming into evidence).

Saipov's lawyer says, No cross

 AUSA reads for jury the transcript of previous Saipov statement, I don't see Allah in this courtroom.

Judge Broderick says, "Sure."

Next up: Medical examiner, lengthy stipulation about cause of death.

Saipov continues, now 5:30 pm - Judge Broderick asks if he should dismiss Juror 37 who has to leave the case by March 22.

Federal Defender Dalack says the Judge can't carry over alternates to the death penalty phase - but also opposes Juror 37 being let go.

The Federal Defenders made this argument in a January 16, 2023 filing that Kurt noticed and wrote up. It would come up again, when Juror 4 had a family emergency - see below.

Saipov charge conference continues, 6:15 pm.

Federal Defenders say you can't charge with Saipov with offering himself as personnel, and also with the attack.

Judge: I will include "a person who provides services" as part of the charge.

* * *

On January 24, the US and defense presented closing arguments, then Judge Broderick solicited more submissions for his jury instruction. Thread here:

OK - US closing statement in liability phase.

Assistant US Attorney: As bikes lay mangled, as the FBI rushed to the scene, as the deceased were ID-ed, as the dust settled, questions emerged. Who did it? How? And third, why?

Now you know the answers. Saipov did it, with a 6000 pound truck, to become a part of ISIS...

AUSA: Saipov sat in the hospital and he knew that his mission was accomplished. Eight were dead. He was the newest recruit. He smiled when he confessed.

Now, the closing statement for Sayfullo Saipov.

Federal Defender Patton: Let's walk through the facts, what he actually did, what he said about it in the interrogation in the hospital, and what was found in his possession. Mr. Saipov rented a truck... He veered onto the bike path, he killed people, he slammed into that school bus. When the truck is wrecked, he gets out with 2 fake guns. He doesn't run away. Here are images [video is shown]

With Federal Defender distinguishing ISIS membership from "Soldiers of the Caliphate," Judge Broderick tells the jury to take a break.

They're still at it at 5:32 pm - Judge Broderick ruling on (and rejecting) an instruction for his jury charge. Then: we will get the parties a clean version, and go from there.

* * *

On January 25, Judge Broderick hears argument on, and then reads to the jury, his legal charge for this first stage. He issued a 33-page order largely denying Saipov's motions regarding any second phase, but granted one in part, on Factors, specifically the "Future Dangerousness" Non-statutory Factor.

Of this, Judge Broderick wrote that "the parties are directed to meet and confer about how to proceed on this factor. Either the government will be granted leave to file an amended notice reflecting the more narrowly tailored version of the Future Dangerouness factor as limited to what Saipov can do in prison, or, the parties will inform me that the Future Dangerousness factor will be retained and propose a limiting instruction to the jury."

January 25 overtime thread:

Judge Broderick emerges and takes the bench at 5:40 pm. He says he's sending the six alternates home - and says the 12 "real" jurors indicated they weren't ready to leave for the evening yet.

"But I believe that's imminent." Now he tells alternates to come tomorrow.

Judge Broderick: We have a note. Questions from jury: is the defense contending that the defendant committed the crime but was charged with the wrong crimes? What if he flew to ISIS and got an ID card? If we found him not guilty, would he be re-charged?

In the courtroom: looks of surprise. Some apparent eye-rolling. A laugh?

Judge Broderick (to the parties) Feel free to take pictures of the note with your phones. I assume jurors want to go home. But I don't know that. These questions are like a conversation, not questions about the evidence.

Federal Defender: Let's send jurors home.

And then on January 26 after more questions, the 28 guilty verdicts with the penalty phase to come.

On January 26, Saipov was found guilty on all counts, after jury questions about whether he did it to join or advance himself in ISIS or not. That will be a major issue, along with any mitigation, in the penalty phase to come.

The US Attorney's Office said in a statement that Saipov "was found guilty of eight counts of murder in aid of racketeering activity, which carry a penalty of death or life in prison, eight counts of assault with a dangerous weapon and attempted murder in aid of racketeering activity, which carry a maximum penalty of 20 years in prison, 10 counts of attempted murder in aid of racketeering activity, which carry a maximum penalty of 10 years in prison, one count of providing and attempting to provide material support to a designated foreign terrorist organization, which carries a maximum penalty of life in prison, and one count of violence and destruction of motor vehicles, which carries a penalty of death or life in prison. The penalty phase is scheduled to begin on February 6, 2023."

After the verdict, Saipov's lead counsel wrote to Judge Broderick: "We write in anticipation of tomorrow's conference. The defense intends to address with the Court the issues that remain outstanding from its omnibus challenge to the government's penalty phase evidence, particularly with respect to the victim impact and future danger aggravators."

On January 30, the US argued to Judge Broderick in writing that they want the jury to see Saipov's note to Ruslan Maratovich Asainov, now on trial in EDNY for providing material support to ISIS. "The Government does not presently intend to elicit testimony regarding Asainov's ISIS affiliation." Presently...

On February 1, the US Attorney's Office wrote to Judge Broderick that they would start their penalty phase case on February 13, through February 21. Then the defense from February 22. Judge Broderick ruled:

"ORDER as to Sayfullo Habibullaevic Saipov. The Government Wall Team and Defense counsel shall meet tomorrow at 11:00 AM in Courtroom 24B. Following a finding in open-court, the conference will proceed in camera (Signed by Judge Vernon S. Broderick on 2/1/2023)."

Inner City Press went. Judge Broderick read a script about the presumption in criminal cases of openness to the public and press - then said because this discussion implicated defense strategy about ADX Florence in Colorado, it would be sealed, *in camera*, in the jury room. Federal Defenders asked to bring in an additional person, which was allowed, with some sort of summary expected on February 4.

* * *

On February 8, Judge Broderick held a proceeding and issued rulings, including these:

Judge Broderick: We have reached all jurors, they can sit Friday. Juror 37, who is Juror 1, has an appointment on Feb 23, so we can't start until 11 am. I'll let the jurors know. Juror 531 called chambers and was rude and inappropriate, about sitting on February 27.

Judge Broderick: I was going to pick up the phone and speak to Juror 531, who is Juror 13 in the box - but it was not the time. It will be, on Monday. I'm going to speak with him about it....

Judge Broderick is back and says, I'm going to read my decision from inside the witness box so I can remove my mask. I took a COVID test, but we had that occur earlier in the case. So to remove any concerns, let me get in the box. [He does]

Judge Broderick: I exclude the government's video [of kids' reaction] - they are in the school yards. But from 24 to 27 seconds, it shows the truck. Therefore that can come in, on the selection of site for acts of terrorism factor.

Judge Broderick: I am allowing in testimony about the psychological impacts. And, no court has excluded financial impact testimony from a death penalty case and I decline to do so here. I will read the jury a curative instruction.

On February 12, on the eve of the death penalty phase of the trial, the US Attorney's Office filed opposition to a defense video deposition:

"The Government writes in response to the defense requests (i) for a video deposition, pursuant to Federal Rule of Criminal Procedure 15, of Khalfan Khamis Mohamed, an inmate at the United States Penitentiary Florence – Administrative Maximum Facility ("ADX"); or (ii) in the alternative, for Mohamed to testify at trial by two-way videoconference from ADX. (Defense Letter Dated February 8, 2023 ("Ltr."); February 8,

2023 Transcript ("Tr.") 1858–71).1 The Government objects to these requests. Because Mohamed is available to testify in court, and because his proposed testimony is largely irrelevant and otherwise cumulative, there is no lawful basis for him to testify remotely. He should instead testify in the same manner as every other witness in this case: in person and in court."

* * *

On February 13, the death penalty phase began. Inner City Press was there, live tweeted thread here.

Judge Broderick: I find that Mr. Mohamed [Super-max inmate Khalfan Khamis Mohamed] is not unavailable, so he should be subject to cross-examination, and be transported here.

[After argument]

Judge Broderick: I will allow Mr. Mohamed to testify to CC-TV. But I do not want the government to be prejudiced. The parties should confer about the scope of the testimony. Will he testify about his experience as an inmate there?

Defense: Yes.

As Judge Broderick goes back into jury room to dismiss juror 531, Kurt (and probably they) noted this: "Multiple pedestrians were struck and a cyclist was dragged by a U-Haul truck in Brooklyn Monday morning. The truck hit people near 5th Ave & Bay Ridge Parkway at 11 am.

Judge Broderick is back.

He asks, Do the parties want me to say anything about Juror 13/531?

They defer to the Court Judge Broderick: I propose to say, You may have notice Juror 13 is no longer part of the jury. Don't speculate why. We're just waiting for the jury

Jury entering!

Judge Broderick: Welcome back. You may have noticed Juror 13 is no longer on the jury.

You should not speculate as to why this is the case. Now I have questions: have you read or seen anything about this case? Have you done any research or posted online?

Judge Broderick: No raised hands? Good. You have convicted Mr. Saipov and we are about to begin the penalty phase on Counts 1-8 and 28, on whether death is appropriate.

Now prosecutors are showing photo of Martin and asking, "How did your husband react when you gave birth to Martin?"

A: He almost fainted.

Assistant US Attorney: How often do you think about your husband?

A: Every day. Our kids, they need to talk about it. Now I have to honor this family, this history, to instill his values.

AUSA: No further questions.

Not surprisingly, for this widow, Federal Defenders have no cross-examination questions.

Judge Broderick, at 4:30 pm, declares afternoon break. Meanwhile on 14th floor, big crowd gathered for a sentencing, delayed by trial

Judge Broderick is back: "We are going to be able to go to 5:30, Ms. Rodriguez has confirmed it."

Next witness is Rachel Pharn, hit by Saipov's truck.

AUSA: Please describe your injuries.

Pharn: My foot and ankle were broken, and my shoulder was injured.

Again no cross-examination, of Mr. Pharn.

Now witness Ariel of Argentina. Prosecutors show selfie video of them happily biking - before the (targeted) crash.

At 5: 30 pm, Judge Broderick lets the jurors go for the day. AUSA says there is an issue to discuss.

On February 14, in Day 2 of the death penalty phase, the government showed video from inside the Metropolitan Correctional Center (the type of video it did NOT have for Jeffrey Epstein), on a day the BOP official said Saipov spoke of having a guard beheaded. Thread here:

OK - Day 2 with friend of 1 of 8 deceased victims on the witness stand.

Jury entering!

Judge Broderick: Good morning. We will continue with Mr. Benvenuto on the stand.

AUSA: What impact has Hernan's death had on you?

Benvenuto: It is hard to express. It is a pain that will mark me the rest of my life.

Now the prosecutors put into evidence a photo of a tattoo the witness got, about deceased Hernan.

Saipov's Federal Defenders are opposing admission of information about the victims, saying it enflames the emotions of the jurors "in violation of the 8th Amendment."

AUSA: Mr. Saipov drove over her. We are putting in a photograph of her in a wheelchair

Next witness is Bureau of Prisons' Rosa Proto.

AUSA: What is the purpose of the BOP?

Proto: To protect inmates, staff, and society.

AUSA: Where you in charge of the SAM Unit at the MCC?

Proto: Yes.

AUSA: Where is the MCC?

Proto: 150 Park Row.

AUSA: And what are SAMs?

Proto: Special Administrative Measures. They are decided by the Attorney General.

AUSA: Did you deal with Mr. Saipov in the MCC on December 18, 2019?

Proto: Yes. He had a social call.

AUSA: Did you go to his cell?

Proto: Yes, with an officer, because Mr. Saipov had covered the security camera in his cell.

AUSA: What did Mr. Saipov say to you?

Proto: That the officer during the night was an animal, and that he would not uncover the camera until the officer's head was chopped off. The officer had woken him up in the night, he said.

Now prosecutors are playing for the jurors a video from inside the Metropolitan Correctional Center, outside Saipov's cell on Dec 18, 2019.

[Hard not to think, at least for Kurt: *they have this but no video of Jeffrey Epstein's fateful night*.]

Cross examination:

Federal Defender: Visitors in the SAMs unit cannot touch the prisoner, even with paper, right?

Proto: No.

Federal Defender: And --

Judge Broderick: I think she said "no."

FD: Thank you. Let me clean that up. Is it correct that contact is prohibited?

Proto: Yes.

Federal Defender: In the SAMs Unit, the officers checked on inmates during the night with the flashlight, right?

Proto: Yes.

Federal Defender: And to leave the cell, the escort was one lieutenant and two officers, correct?

Proto: Yes.

Next witness is Juan Pablo Trevisan, from Argentina. He was biking that day...

AUSA: What were your injuries?

Trevisan: Fractured wrist, nerve in elbow.

AUSA: I'd like to start with your group of friends...

Prosecutors show jury Trevisan's video of the group biking through Central Park on Halloween 2017.

AUSA: Why did you record these videos?

Trevisan: We watched them later. We put them on a WhatsApp group.

Just before 5:30, Judge Broderick lets the jurors go, after asking the parties to at least list exhibits they may object to.

* * *

On February 15, a full day of victim impact statements, with no cross-examination by Federal Defenders, thread here:

OK - Day 3 of death penalty phase with wife of deceased Hernan Ferruchi, Vera Dargoltz, on the witness stand.

Assistant US Attorney: How did you hear about the incident in New York?

Ms. Dargoltz: My father-in-law called and asked if I'd heard from Hernan. I asked, Why? He said, No, nothing. Then he said, there had been an attack, in Manhattan.

Ms. Dargoltz: So I turned on the TV, and saw the bikes, and I called the consulate. They said they had no news about Hernan. But then...

 Not surprisingly, no cross-examination of widow by Saipov's Federal Defenders.

Next witness is Lina Ferruchi, Hernan's daughter, now 20. She describes Hernan "dancing to the YMCA song, with a construction helmet on." She is going into psychology.

Now on the witness stand is the mother of Nicholas Cleves, who was 23 when he was killed by Saipov while riding a CitiBike on West Side Highway bike path.

AUSA: Were there law enforcement officers at your apartment?

A: Yes.

 Now after a relative of deceased bike path victim Diego Angelini, the prosecution's next witnesses are Luciana Paula Martinez and now Martin Marro, who acknowledges that the injuries he suffered made him irritable at home and work.

* * *

On February 16, the victim impacts statements continued, with tears. The Federal Defenders put in a letter demanded to see the "scripts" of the victims, in advance, to "allow the parties to address objections in advance of the testimony." Because they don't want to cross-examine crying survivors and victim relatives in front of the jury....

On February 17, the Federal Defenders filed a motion to dismiss based on the victim statements being too prejudicial. FD cited the "dramatic and emotional testimony of Alexander Naessens, Ann-Laure Decadt's widower and Lieve Wyseur, Ms. Decadt's mother."

The Federal Defenders say that "the penalty phase of a federal capital proceeding is not the forum for victims to freely express their emotions or, in Ms. Wyseur's case, vent their (understandable) rage and torment."

* * *

But in the penalty phase, on February 21 members of the media were not allowed into the courtroom, only to elsewhere in the courthouse where a feed shows only part of the courtroom. Inner City Press, the first of many media in opposition, wrote to Judge Broderick, here

Here's from the day's testimony, after which Judge Broderick said the press can have a bench in the back, thread:

OK - now with media excluded from courtroom in death penalty phase in US v. Saipov, week's 1st witness is the sister of victim Kristin Lin, with a prepared statement.

Sister: Kristin was on the special needs school bus that day. She used to walk our dog along that bike path.

Next witness is Ivan Brajckovic. AUSA: Remind the jury, were you present on the bike path with your friends from Argentina?

Brajckovic: Yes. My friend Ariel Erlij was killed. 40 years of friendship... (He sobs; jurors' reactions cannot be described.)

Next witness is Pabla Pereyra, wife of victim Ariel Erlij. She was 16 when they met; 23 when they married. AUSA: How was your wedding? Pabla Pereyra: It was the best wedding of the year. [Photos shown; reactions unseen.]

Next witness in courtroom with media excluded is mother of Saipov victim Darren Drake.

AUSA: Who is in this photo?

Ms. Drake: Darren Drake. The photo was from 2017. He was 32, when he died... He played football, as a lineman, but mowing people down wasn't in him.

Ms. Drake: Darren was our only child. We miss him terribly. We have set up a foundation in his name, for scholarships to trade school.

AUSA: No further question.

Judge Broderick: Cross-examination?

FD Dalack: No, your Honor. [Can't see jury response about Drake.]

Next US witness is Darren Drake's cousin, who says he loved singing karaoke, they'd go bar to bar in Hoboken. His death, she says, has changed everything for her. Impossible to see response of jurors. Will Judge Broderick address the pending motions before 5:30 pm?

Judge Broderick is letting the jurors go for the day. He says he'll have "brief comments for the gallery." But first, AUSA Houle says the defense didn't give the prosecution any notes about preparing the Saipov family members for testimony.

Judge Broderick: Folks in the gallery, thanks for your cooperation. What I would say is that we do have a full house. I'm going to instruct that the bench all the way in the back is going to be reserved for members of the press. I want to notify you. OK. Adjourned.

On February 22, there was a single witness, about ADX Florence. Thread here:

OK- now death penalty phase with media semi-restored to courtroom, witness is about Special Administrative Procedures

Q: What is the ratio of inmates to staff?

A: In each unit, 25 inmates to 7 staff on the floor.

Q: How many hours a day in the cell?

A: 22 to 23 hours a day.

Defense Exhibit 17 is shown: concrete bed and shelf, thin window.

The cell has a cigarette lighter; the witness says "we no longer sell tobacco and that lighter has been deactivated."

A: The window is 5 by 38 inches. They can use the toilet when they want but we limit the number of flushes. And not only to conserve water.
In H Unit, we apply hand restraints. We ask the inmate to back up with their hands out --

Q: What's this?

A: Solid outer door looking into a cell...
That's the TV, we give them one, we have 16 channels of content. If they break it, no new one unless they pay. We do not show local channels, since staff live locally and we do not want inmates learning about them. But they get ESPN, for example.

[Kurt perked up as he live-tweeted the testimony - ESPN? The ever-expanding cable monopolist of every sport on earth? Sometimes, like in college football bowl season, Kurt's lack of cable and ESPN got to him. But he'd be damned if he would pay, from what his court reporting brought in on Patreon. And the corporate courts that made pirating ESPN another form of crime.]

Q: In H unit, have you had inmates convicted of terrorism?

A: Yes.

Q: In H Unit, have you found a cell phone?

A: No.

Q: Has there ever been a serious attack in H Unit?

A: No.

Q: An escape?

A: No.

Q: So is it safe to say that H Unit has successfully held people convicted of terrorism?

A: Yes.

AUSA: Sidebar?

Now cross examination of ADX Florence Bureau of Prisons witness:

AUSA: How many inmates get released from H Unit?

A: About three a year.

AUSA: And they can earn their way out of ADX altogether, right?

A: They can.

AUSA: And inmates can get their SAMs loosened through an administrative process, correct?

A: Yes. They have had gotten access to more TV channels, communications with lawyers who do not yet represent them.

It's over for the day - a single witness, all about H Unit in ADX Florence, Colorado.

* * *

On Sunday, February 26, the US wrote to Judge Broderick asking him to allow a rebuttal witness:

"The Government writes in further support of the admissibility of the anticipated testimony of Bureau of Prisons Lieutenant James Dupree. 1 Below, the Government details defense argument and evidence from the penalty phase that confirm why the proposed testimony is admissible in rebuttal. In opening statements, the defense argued that the jury should sentence the defendant to life imprisonment based in part on the defense's characterization of the defendant's future conditions of confinement and how these conditions would prevent him from communicating with others unsupervised: - "[Chris Synsvoll] will tell you about H Unit and assure you that the Federal Bureau of

Prisons can and will control Saipov." (Trial Transcript ("Tr.") 2023:21-22). - "You will hear what Saipov's life will be like at the H Unit of ADX and learn that he will lose almost everything that makes life sweet. He will spend at least 23 hours in his cell alone." (Tr. 2023:23-25)...

The defendant has, however, attempted to evade these very restrictions in the past. The Government anticipates that Lieutenant Dupree would testify that on or about February 6, 2022, the defendant gave Lieutenant Dupree a bag of candy and asked him to give it to another inmate, Ruslan Maratovich Asainov, who is also subject to SAMs. 2 When Lieutenant Dupree noticed that the bag of candy was open, he looked inside and found a note. He seized the note, which was written partially in English and partially in Uzbek."

On Monday, February 27, Judge Broderick docketed: "ORDER as to Sayfullo

Habibullaevic Saipov. In accordance with my request on February 3, February 14, and February 23, 2023, it is hereby ORDERED that by end of day on Tuesday, February 28, 2023, the Defense provide me with the number of people in the following categories for each year beginning with 2018 through the present who have worked on this case: - Lawyers; - Volunteer attorneys; - Other, non-legal volunteers; - Paralegals. As I indicated on the record, I am only asking for the number of individuals and not any names. If the Defense believes this information is attorney work product or otherwise confidential, Defense may file a redacted version of this list on the docket."

Why would the number of Defenders be confidential?

On February 28 as part of the defense case, an expert on Central Asia testified.
Thread here:

Jury entering!

Judge Broderick: The defense should call its next witness.

It's Noah Tucker - The Oxus Society for Central Asian Affairs

Assistant US Attorney: Did you review the ISIS propaganda on Mr. Saipov's phone in this case?

Noah Tucker: I did. There is pseudo-news, and direct ISIS recruiting materials, mostly from Telegram channels. On some videos, ISIS left in the concluding credits, for example asking the viewer to donate to Amnesty International. They like that. They think it makes it look more legitimate.

Now defense expert Tucker is being cross examined.

AUSA: Your research has shown that in "social media communities," like Uzbek Facebook, there was an anti-ISIS message being promoted, correct?

Tucker: Yes. Not everyone stood by and watched it happen, the spread of ISIS ideology.

Redirect:

Tucker: The Uzbek government is not effective in combatting terrorism, it does not distinguish between real terrorists and devout people. They make up Jihadist groups.

Judge Broderick lets the jury go - then tells counsel that he'd like to tell the jurors that next week they'll hear summations and get the case (to decide on death penalty).

Now as lawyers' arguments continue, the Federal Defenders say they waive the appearance of Mr. Saipov - and he says, in English, "I want to leave."

Judge Broderick: Marshals, you may transport Mr. Saipov.

Federal Defender Dalack: El Chapo was flown out quickly after conviction --

Judge Broderick: That may have had something to do with him having escaped with a motorcycle and a tunnel, and law enforcement shutting down the Brooklyn Bridge during his transport.

FD: I'm not trying to compare the two.

Judge Broderick: The parties should confer on a possible stipulation [about administrative punishment of Saipov in prison for infractions] and if you can't decide, I'll do it tomorrow. Adjourned.

* * *

On March 1, the defense rested its case, *sans* Saipov. Inner City Press live tweeted here:

OK - now the defense puts on a relative about Sayfullo Saipov coming to US from Uzbekistan on green card.

Mother: Sayfullo decided to drive trucks and took lessons to do so.

Federal Defender: Were you able to stay in touch with him?

Mother: Yes, he would call me while driving. He got married in 2012 and had three children.

 Judge Broderick asks Saipov if he'll want to attend, on Monday, the jury charge conference in his death penalty case. No, he does not.

He has better things to do, apparently.

Jury entering!

This is the defense's last witness: Steven Wein of the US Marshals Service.

Federal Defender: Do you drive Mr. Saipov to court?

Wein: I do. He travels alone, under the SAMs.

 After a brief direct of US Marshal Wein, no

cross examination by the prosecutors. Judge Broderick asks jurors to step out (again) for a moment, and not to discuss the case.

Judge: Mr. Saipov, do you want to testify?

Saipov: Not now.

The trial is ending...

Judge Broderick to the jury: Come back on Tuesday for summations. There are cookies in the jury room and you can take them with you. Never say the government didn't give you anything.

On March 3, the US Attorney's Office wrote to Judge Broderick seeking to preclude the defense from arguing in closing that the jury should choose a "civilized sense of justice" over "barbarism."

Federal Defenders also wrote in, protesting the US' proposed verdict form and proposed penalty-phase instructions, and submitting its own in advance of the charge conference set for March 6.

On March 6 at the charge conference, EDNY cases and legislative history were argued, thread here:

Judge Broderick: Info from Mr. Saipov's phones was utilized in both phases... Any objection to this revision to the charge?

AUSA: No.

Federal Defenders: It seems unclear if Corrections Officers are law enforcement officers for this purpose.

Judge: I'll take it out of the charge.

After Judge Broderick scheduled an unrelated criminal case Inner City Press is also covering, here... The charge conference continues, with the Federal Defenders reiterating motions about aggravating factors they first made back in... 2018.

Judge: Duly noted.

Judge Broderick asks what was done in the EDNY case of US v Wilson.

Federal Defenders propose telling jurors to imagine Saipov's (and his victims'?) religions reversed, citing legislative history of Federal Death Penalty Act.

On March 7, the US Attorney's Office closing, thread here:

Assistant US Attorney Houle: The defendant murdered his victims while destroying a motor vehicle. The defendant engaged in substantial planning of this act of terrorism... On his phone is evidence of his searches about Halloween in NYC. Here is the video of him walking calmly out of the Home Depot... With the clerk he talked about the beaches in Tampa. He is callous.

AUSA: This defendant deserves the ultimate sentence, a sentence of death. Murder is always terrible. But he chose to murder multiple people. That is what this factor is aimed at. He stole eight lives.

AUSA: His father could not bear to look at the body of his son, Darren Drake. Jimmy used to drive him to the PATH train. Now he drives around twice a day, fleeing his grief. Barbara said, We don't look forward to anything anymore. The defendant chose this...

AUSA: This is Nicholas Cleve at a TED Talk, looking like he was at a rock concern. He was so excited. He said he would design a one-dollar computer.

[Now AUSA shows video of school bus Saipov hit with his Home Depot pickup truck]

AUSA: The Hudson River bike path is a special place. People thought it was secure.

The defendant attacked that. For all of these reasons, the most severe punishment is warranted in this case. The defendant is likely to commit future violence in prison.

AUSA: The defendant believes he is a victorious soldier who will "return home a winner." He believes there are big things ahead for him, that it's why he survived. He's screaming about killing people. Three BOP officers told you of threats.

AUSA: Defendant covered up his camera. In ADX, inmates have gotten razor blades in the H Unit....

Now Judge Broderick calls the (more than an hour) lunch break for the jurors, telling them to report to him if anyone approaches them.

With jury out of the room, Federal Defender objects to AUSA just now telling jurors about the two inmates with razors in ADX Florence, as a reason to execute Saipov.

Judge Broderick overrules the objection.

Later on March 7, the defense's closing, and US Attorney's Office's rebuttal, resumed thread here

They're back for Saipov's Federal Defender's closing.

FD Patton: It is not necessary to kill Sayfullo Saipov. By your verdict last month you have guaranteed that he will be sent away to one of the most isolated spots on the planet. Decide for life.

FD Patton: Meeting death with more death is not the answer. Nothing we do can undo what Mr. Saipov did. But dying in a faraway prison, forgotten, may be worse than dying as a martyr. The law never requires death no matter how horrific the crime.

FD Patton: This is a moral decision --

AUSA: Objection!

Judge: It's argument, I'll allow it. Proceed.

FD Patton: Let's turn now to where Mr. Saipov is headed. It's in the high desert. There are 3 showers a week, and 2 calls a month.

FD Patton: There's 9 inch TV with basic channels... Mr. Saipov's life will be regulated, he will make no choices. He will be in a cage by himself and may be given a ball to hit against the wall. Here's the library: a non-Internet computer with a legal database.

FD Patton: In the 21 years of ADX, there have been two razor blades found, in 2003 and 2018. And once someone figured out how to distill alcohol from some of the food they served. They stopped serving that food.

FD Patton: Sayfullo Saipov hasn't actually harmed anyone in five and a half years. You heard from our expert Noah Tucker... After Halloween, Sayfullo's father was detained in

Uzbekistan for 15 days... Your Honor, may we take a break?

Judge: Yes.

FD Patton is ending his closing with a quote from "Just Mercy" by Bryan Stevenson.

Now the US rebuttal by AUSA Jason Richman:

AUSA Richman: The defense asked you to choose life. It was Saipov who chose death. For eight people. So this is not just about adding up mitigating and aggravating factors. When the defendant shows you who he is, believe him. He can sit and plan just like he did on October 31 --

Federal Defender: Objection!

Judge Broderick: It's argument. I'll allow it.

AUSA Richman: People do get off of SAMs. No one said he seemed possessed --

Federal Defender: Objection!

Judge Broderick: Overruled. Continue.

AUSA Richman: Noah Tucker never met Saipov. The pain his family showed? He himself caused it. Don't the deaths he caused call for more than the minimum?

Federal Defender: Objection!

Judge Broderick. Yes. Move on.

AUSA: He asked to hang an ISIS flag in his hospital room.

Judge Broderick: Jurors, tomorrow we will have the jury charge. It will take several hours. Then you will deliberate [on the death penalty].

With jury gone, Federal Defenders specify their objections, that AUSA Richman said they can't guarantee Saipov won't be a danger, arguing that it shifts the burden. A mistrial is again requested.

Judge Broderick : I deny the motion for a

mistrial. Let's discuss the remaining jury charge issues.

Federal Defender: The Marshals' transport is here and Mr. Saipov would like to leave.

Judge: Do you want to leave?

Saipov: Yes I want to leave.

[He does.]

Judge Broderick: It's not quite over yet, but I want to thank everyone for their work on this over the last five years. I apologize for my levity - see you tomorrow.

On March 8, after more argument, there was the jury charge, beginning:

"1 Introductory Instruction Members of the jury, it is again my duty to instruct you as to the law applicable to the sentencing phase of this case. The sole question before you is whether the defendant, Sayfullo Saipov,

should be sentenced for his capital offenses to
(1) the death penalty; or (2) lifetime
imprisonment without the possibility of
release. The selection between these very
serious punishments is yours and yours alone
to make. If you determine, as to a particular
count, that Mr. Saipov should be sentenced to
death, or instead to life imprisonment without
possibility of release, the Court is required to
impose whichever sentence you choose as to
that count. That sentence is final. There is no
parole in the federal system, so a life sentence
means exactly that – Mr. Saipov will spend
the rest of his life in prison and never be
released. A death sentence means that Mr.
Saipov will be executed. You have previously
found Mr. Saipov guilty of Counts 1-8,
murder for the purpose of gaining entrance to
ISIS, and Count 28, Damage or Destruction
of a Motor Vehicle, in the Indictment, which
I read to you at the start of this penalty phase.
These are the capital counts at issue here, and
you must approach the sentencing decision
before you, separately, as to each count and,

of course, with an open mind. I cannot stress to you enough the importance of your giving careful and thorough consideration to all the evidence. Regardless of any opinion you may have as to what the law may be or should be, it would be a violation of your oaths as jurors to base your sentencing decision upon any view of the law other than that which is given to you in these instructions. The instructions I am giving you now are a complete set of instructions on the law applicable to the sentencing decision as to the defendant, Mr. Saipov. 2 During your deliberations, you should rely on these instructions. I have also prepared a Special Verdict Form that you must complete. The form details the findings you must make and will serve as a guide to your deliberations. Although Congress has left it to you, the jury, to decide Mr. Saipov's proper punishment, it has narrowed and channeled your discretion in specific ways, particularly by making you consider and weigh "aggravating" and "mitigating" factors present in this case. Aggravating factors are certain specified factors that could support a death sentence. By contrast, mitigating factors are any factors that would suggest, for any individual juror, that life imprisonment without possibility of release is the more appropriate punishment. Of course, your task is not simply to decide what aggravating and mitigating factors exist here, if any. Rather, you are called upon to evaluate any such factors and to make a unique, individualized moral choice between the death penalty and life in prison without the possibility of release. The law never requires that any defendant found guilty of committing capital murder must be sentenced to death. Rather, the law requires that you consider whether all the aggravating factor or factors found to exist sufficiently outweigh all the mitigating factor or factors found to exist to justify a sentence of death, or, in the absence of a mitigating factor, whether the aggravating factor or factors alone are sufficient to justify a sentence of death. If you find no aggravating factors have been proven beyond a reasonable doubt, the defendant will be sentenced to life imprisonment without the possibility of release. During the Government's rebuttal summation, it mentioned the concept of a minimum sentence. There is no evidence in the record of a minimum sentence absent aggravating factors. A finding of aggravating factors does not make a death sentence required or presumed or make consideration of mitigating factors any less important or required...

"If and only if you unanimously find that the Government has proven, beyond a reasonable doubt, that the defendant was at least eighteen years of age and the existence of at least one of the four preliminary intent factors as to a particular capital count, you must then proceed to determine whether the Government has proven, beyond a reasonable doubt, the existence of any of the following statutory aggravating factors with respect to that same count: 1. The death or injury resulting in death of the victim or victims

(Diego Enrique Angelini, Nicholas Cleves, Ann-Laure Decadt, Darren Drake, Ariel Erlij, Hernan Ferruchi, Hernan Diego Mendoza, and Alejandro Damian Pagnucco) occurred during the commission or attempted commission of the offense of damage and destruction of a motor vehicle under Title 18, United States Code, Section 33. 2. Mr. Saipov committed the offense after substantial planning and premeditation to cause the death of a person or commit an act of terrorism. 3. Mr. Saipov intentionally killed or attempted to kill more than one person in a single criminal episode. At this point the law directs you to consider and decide, separately as to each of the capital counts for which you have unanimously found that the defendant was at least eighteen years of age and the existence of at least one preliminary intent factor, the existence or non- existence of the statutory aggravating factors specifically claimed by the Government. You are reminded that to find the existence of a statutory aggravating factor as to a particular count, your decision must be unanimous and beyond a reasonable doubt. Any finding that one or more of these factors has been proven must be based on Mr. Saipov's personal actions and intent. In the event that you unanimously find, beyond a reasonable doubt, that a particular statutory aggravating factor exists as to one or more, but not all, of the capital counts for which you have found that the defendant was at least eighteen years of age and the existence of at least one preliminary intent factor, you are to indicate that finding in the appropriate box provided on the Special Verdict Form, and also identify on the line provided, by count number, the particular count or counts as to which you find the statutory aggravating factor applies. If you do not unanimously find that a particular statutory aggravating factor has been proved beyond a reasonable doubt with respect to any of the capital counts you are considering, you should mark the appropriate box provided on the Special Verdict Form. For any capital count for which you unanimously found that the defendant was at least eighteen years of age and the existence of at least one preliminary intent factor, if you do not also unanimously find as to that same count the existence of at least one statutory aggravating factor, then your deliberative task as to that count will be over, and the Court will impose a sentence on that count of life imprisonment without the possibility of release. Section III, Part B of the Special Verdict Form provides a space for you to indicate the counts, if any, for which you have not unanimously found that the Government has proven beyond a reasonable doubt the existence of any statutory aggravating factor.

" Mr. Saipov committed the offense to support and further the ideological goals of the Islamic State of Iraq and al-Sham ("ISIS"), a terrorist organization that has as one of its goals to kill U.S. nationals around the world. 4. Mr. Saipov is likely to commit criminal acts of violence in the future such that he poses a continuing and serious threat to the lives and safety of others. The Government claims this is demonstrated by, among other things, his commission of the acts of violence charged in the Indictment, his stated intent to continue his attack in New York City had his truck not been rendered inoperable, and his continued support for the radical terrorist activities and goals of ISIS, which include the killing of U.S. nationals. In deciding whether this alleged aggravating factor has been proved, you must understand and accept that if he is not sentenced to death, Mr. Saipov will be in prison for the rest of his life with no possibility of release. You must consider only the danger that Mr. Saipov may present in prison. The government must prove more than just that Mr. Saipov remains a danger or a threat; rather, you must agree unanimously that the Government has proven beyond a reasonable doubt that Mr. Saipov is likely to commit criminal acts of violence in the future in prison such that he poses a continuing and serious threat to the lives and safety of others. 5. Mr. Saipov targeted the bike path on the West Side Highway on Halloween because he intended to maximize the devastation to civilians and in an attempt to instill fear in New Yorkers and tourists who use the bike path. 6. Mr. Saipov demonstrated a lack of remorse for the offense in the days and months following his crimes."

Then deliberations began with two notes (and two "no" answers). The jury was let go after 5:30 and will resume on March 9. March 8 thread here:

OK - Judge hearing yet more arguments before having the jury come in. Now Judge Broderick says he's going to finalize and print out the jury charge. The jurors are still in the bullpen and he says he'll see if they can have lunch and then listen for two to three hours "which is what it's going to take."

Finally the jury is being brought it to hear the charge. First Judge Broderick asks Saipov to confirm that he waives his presence for arguments, since he was praying and eating lunch - the lunch the Federal Defenders briefed if not cooked for him?

Near 1:30 pm, Judge Broderick starts reading the 43-page jury charge, the final version of which has been docketed - Kurt immediately uploaded it to DocumentCloud then tweeted it.

There's also the 18-page verdict form to be giving out after the charge. In the half-full Saipov courtroom after the charge, there are two quartets of lawyers as two US Marshals stand ready to bring Saipov back in from the holding cell if there is a note. Too early for a verdict...

Can - and, separately, will - the Saipov jurors discuss the *method* that would be used for execution, and DOJ moratorium?   Here comes Judge Broderick back to the bench.

Judge Broderick: So I will tell them it is inappropriate and they should not discuss it. But my understanding is that in New York, it would not necessarily be lethal injection, right? Since NYS does not have the death penalty, the decision on method would fall to me?

[Somewhere on Park Row, Michael Randall Long was beside himself. It wasn't that Judge Broderick would, like a king, decide the method of execution. Rather, he would name as the model to follow that of a state that still has the death penalty, at least on the books.]

Judge Broderick: It's concerning that they're starting off with an incorrect assumption. But I'm sticking my head where it need not go. I'll call out the jury and read them the response. Let's get the jury.

Jury entering!

Judge Broderick: You asked, Knowing that the method of execution is lethal injection, can we discuss that? Can we mention the current moratorium on executions by Attorney General Merrick Garland? I instruct you these are not proper considerations, do not discuss them.

Now at 5:40 pm, Judge Broderick returns to the bench.

Judge Broderick: Any objection to my calling upstairs the five alternate jurors as well as the twelve?

AUSA: No.

FD: No.

Judge: OK, bring them up. This can be off the record - Mr. Dalack, no letter tonight. I'm up.

Jury entering!

Judge Broderick: Jurors, return tomorrow. Do not discuss the case except when the twelve are together.

[Jurors leave]

Judge Broderick: Yesterday Juror 9 slash 292 used the public restroom. I don't think there was any conversation. But I wanted to inform the parties.

Counsel: Thank you.

All leave.

On March 9 for deliberations, Juror 4 did not come in, due to an undisclosed emergency with a relative (who may or may not be in law enforcement). Judge Broderick noted a Federal Defenders argument, which Kurt first wrote about on January 16, 2023, now with Michael Randall Long adding 18 USC 3593(b)(1)

"(b)Hearing Before a Court or Jury.—If the attorney for the government has filed a notice as required under subsection (a) and the defendant is found guilty of or pleads guilty to an offense described in section 3591, the judge who presided at the trial or before whom the guilty plea was entered, or another judge if that judge is unavailable, shall conduct a separate sentencing hearing to determine the punishment to be imposed. The hearing shall be conducted—

(1) before the jury that determined the defendant's guilt."

Would an appeals court, the Second Circuit if not the current Supreme Court, read that to mean the same exact 12 jurors who found Saipov guilt in the first phase?

With a replacement Juror 4, deliberations started over, including a note with questions about Saipov's threats to behead, and ADX, thread here:

OK - now death penalty deliberations - interruptus? Judge Broderick says Juror 4 has an emergency and can't come in. He has asked parties if an alternate should be called in.

AUSA Houle: Did he say he's not coming back at all, given the situation of his brother?

Judge Broderick: My deputy spoke with him, he was despondent and said would not be coming back. But we could wait and see. I need to check if the relative is in law enforcement... The relative was just found.

AUSA Houle: We'd like a few minutes, given that context.

Judge Broderick: That's fine. I took it Juror 4 was reflecting the seriousness of the communications. That's just my read on it. Juror 4 in the box is Juror 172.

Judge Broderick: Given the defense's previous arguments [that it must be the same 12 jurors in liability and death penalty phases] I anticipate them moving for a mistrial, or a partial mistrial. I want to hear from the parties. I'll give you the time that you need.

Now AUSA Houle says Juror 4 was called by the NYPD and told that his brother had had a heart attack, says the US believes it would be replacement for cause.

Judge Broderick: That NYPD made the call raises the seriousness of a heart attack. Juror 4 was despondent... Juror 4 could be excused for cause, I believe. Waiting is still an option. We have next week, a day we start at 11, another on which Juror 1 slash 37 is not available - and also not available after March 22 or 23. So, anything else on the first issue?

AUSA Houle: What is the defense's position?

FD Patton: We agree.

Judge Broderick: What do the parties think, in the context of the other issue?

FD Patton: For the reasons in our January 16 letter, we move for a mistrial.

Judge Broderick: I deny the motion. Three Circuit courts have considered this issue and found that District Judges can use alternates. I adhere to that. If it comes to that the [2d] Circuit can weigh in.

Judge Broderick: So, they'll have to start their deliberations anew. I'll tell them my instructions on yesterday's questions. I'll tell them, Start anew.

Jury entering! (and alternates)

Judge Broderick: Juror 13 slash 652 is now Juror 4, since Juror 4 has had a family emergency - he's fine, but he won't be returning. Now start again. I have to bring 652 up to speed on the note yesterday, on lethal injection & moratorium.

Judge Broderick: OK, Juror 652 has joined them and they have begun again.

So, the waiting for (next) notes continues.

OK - at 1:19 pm, Judge Broderick is reading out the first note from the "new" jury with Juror 652 as Juror 4.

Judge Broderick: We have a note which reads as follow: on non-statutory aggravating factor 4, is a verbal threat in prison an act of violence? Is the threat to behead an act of violence?

Now at 2:35 pm, the Federal Defenders are at their table, but prosecutors (and Saipov) not in the room.

Saipov is brought back into courtroom. Judge Broderick is reading out loud both sides' proposed answers to the juror questions, on beheading threats and now on how ADX Florence Super Max is run.

Judge Broderick: So I'll answer no, no and you are entitled to consider all the evidence that is before you. I will call the jury in and read the note into the record and the response to each question just after I read it. Ms. Rodriguez, please get the jury.

Judge Broderick: This is off the record. Ms. Houle, you may not see it, but my jeans are not on. [He is robed]

Jury entering!

Judge Broderick: You asked, is a verbal threat in prison a criminal act of violence? The answer is no. Nor is a call for the beheading of corrections officers - it is not a criminal act of violence... You may now return to your deliberations.

[Jury leaves]

Judge: We will give the jurors the form for lunch orders for Monday. Any objection?

Parties: No.

Judge Broderick: Do the parties agree that Ms. Rodriguez can call Juror 4 and tell him that he is excused, and that we wish his brother well? We will do that. Anything else before we continue our waiting?

Parties: No. [So the wait continues]

Now at 4:45 pm Judge Broderick asks for Saipov to be brought in from the holding cell.

Judge: I have received a note from the jury, that they are not going to be able to reach a verdict today. I take that to mean they want to leave and return Monday.

While waiting for the jury to confirm they want to leave for the day and week, Judge

Broderick says, This is probably going to be one of the biggest decisions of their lives, I think they just want to take a little time.

Judge Broderick: They say, We want to break.

Jury entering!

Judge Broderick: So, jurors, enjoy your day off tomorrow. Although it's supposed to rain. So maybe watch something inside. See you Monday.

* * *

Over the weekend Kurt - and Michael Randall Long on Park Row - refused the jury verdict for, including

the term "capital counts" refers to Counts One through Eight and Twenty-Eight, involving the following charges and victims: Murder to Gain Entrance to ISIS Count 1 – Diego Enrique Angelini Count 2 – Nicholas Cleves Count 3 – Ann-Laure Decadt Count 4 – Darren Drake Count 5 – Ariel Erlij Count 6 – Hernan Ferruchi Count 7 – Hernan Diego

Mendoza Count 8 – Alejandro Damian Pagnucco Damage or Destruction of Motor Vehicle Count 28 – All Eight Above-Named Victims Please indicate which, if any, of the following preliminary intent factors you unanimously find that the Government has proven beyond a reasonable doubt. For each of the four factors listed in Part A below, you must mark one of the responses..

Then:

"COUNT ONE We, the jury, unanimously find that a sentence of life in prison without possibility of release is the appropriate sentence for the defendant on Capital Count 1. ❑ We, the jury, unanimously find, for Capital Count 1, that the aggravating factor or factors found to exist sufficiently outweigh the mitigating factor or factors found to exist so that death is the appropriate sentence for the defendant. We vote unanimously that the defendant shall be sentenced to death as to Capital Count 1."

And the same for Counts 2-8 and 28. How would they fill it out? Would they fill it out?

And on Monday, March 13, 2023, for hours there was radio silence. Then, Kurt began live tweeting, thread here:

OK- during death penalty deliberations on Saipov, after hours of radio silence from the jury, now prosecutors Houle & Richmond are at the front table, Saipov led in to the back. Saipov is dressed in red. Still waiting for Judge Broderick. Meanwhile, just docketed is this: "LETTER by USA as to Sayfullo Habibullaevic Saipov dated March 13, 2023 re: Pertinent Authorities for Any Allen Charge Document." The defense objects to an Allen charge.

Judge Broderick takes to the bench. Judge: There is a note from the jury, that they are not able to reach a unanimous verdict. It is signed by Juror 1. I would like to hear from the parties about polling the jury --

FD Levine: We will now file a response to the US   Judge Broderick leaves the bench to read the two sides' letter. Meanwhile, from the US' letter, a case where the judge responded "please continue your deliberations.

Approximately 1 hour later, the jury returned a sentence of death. US v. Fields, 483 F. 3d 313." Now at 2:38 pm with Judge Broderick off the bench reading the parties' Allen charge letters after a jury note that they could not reach unanimity, word comes that a verdict has been reached. Seems strange. Saipov still not back at his seat...

Update: Now Saipov *has* been brought back in by the US Marshals. He's at defense table, smoothing down his hair. Here comes Judge Broderick. Judge: Mr. Saipov, can you hear from the interpreter? Saipov: Yes. AUSA: We are proposing polling at this time...

AUSA: Each jurors should get a piece of paper which asks if they believe that further discussion could lead to a unanimous verdict.

Judge Broderick: What about how long this jury has been out? AUSA: There have been a lot of mitigating and aggravating factors

FD Patton: The US is using a state death penalty case from Louisiana, under the habeus standard. Here, your Honor instructed the jury, If you conclude you are unable to reach a unanimous decision, let me know by note. They did...

FD Patton: What is the point of polling? Whether its 11 to 1, or six to six, the court should not consider that. AUSA Houle: There is also a Fifth Circuit case that acknowledges the benefits of polling.

Judge Broderick: I consider how the charge was formulated

Judge Broderick: I am not going to poll the jury. I do not find it would violate Mr. Saipov's rights. But based on the instructions I gave them, they gave me the same language back. And nothing indicates that they are not fully satisfied. [Phone rings.]

Judge Broderick: Each death penalty case that comes after this one, each Judge is going to have to make his or her decision on whether to poll. Okay. My intention would be to have the alternates come out, then the jury. I'll ask if they've completed the form.

Judge Broderick: Ms. Rodriguez, if you could have the alternate jurors to come up. I'll tell them they can bring their personal items up - any objection? Well, I'll have them keep their belonging downstairs. I'll tell the jurors they can now speak, if they wish...

Update: Judge Broderick has sent the jurors back to each sign the verdict sheet. The remaining alternate jurors are still in the courtroom. The defense lawyers are passing notes among themselves, with Saipov looking on.

Judge Broderick: The jurors have sent another note, that the verdict form as been completed. Judge: Please hand the verdict form to Ms. Rodriguez, please. [Judge Broderick, wearing white COVID mask, flips through the jury form.] Judge: I'm going to read the form

Judge Broderick: So you unanimously find Sayfullo Saipov was 18 years old? Yes is checked. Now Section II. Counts 1-8 and count 28 - we unanimously find that this factor has been proved beyond a reasonable doubt. 2, the same - unanimous finding of yes.

Judge Broderick: 3, you have checked yes, we unanimously find the factor has been proved beyond a reasonable doubt. 4, you have checked We unanimously find it has been proved beyond a reasonable doubt. Part B: any non-unanimous? None, is written.

Judge Broderick: Now, statutory aggravating factors. Part A1, the deaths of Diego Enrique Angelini, Nicholas Cleves, Ann-Laure Decadt, Darren Drake, Ariel Erlij, Hernan Ferruchi, Hernan Diego Mendoza & Alejandro Damian Pagnucco - unanimously, it has been proved   Judge: Again, Part B, any non-unanimous? None is written. Twice.

Now, non-statutory aggravating factors. 4(1), you have unanimously found. And 4(2), on Count 28, you have unanimously found. 4(3), the defendant did this to further ISIS - you have unanimously found

Judge: 4(4), future violence - you have marked, We do NOT unanimously find this has been proved as to any of the capital counts. [Not]

Judge Broderick: 4(5), you have unanimously found the intent to instill fear. And 4(6), lack of remorse, you have unanimously found. Now the mitigating factors. Factor 1, would be incarcerated for life. 12 so find, as on H Unit at ADX Florence: 12

Judge Broderick: Also 12 each on mitigating factors 3 through 26. Mitigating factor 27, are there some who believe life imprisonment is appropriate? Number of jurors: seven.
[Seven]

Judge Broderick: On the rest of item 27, there are not factors filled out. Now Section 6, Determination of Sentence. Count One -

"There is nothing checked off." [Nothing checked off - continues for all other counts]

Judge Broderick: Juror Number 1, does the special verdict form indicate your decision in this case? Yes, your Honor. So say Jurors 2-12.

Judge Broderick: The case is now concluded. You are free to discuss the case if you so choose. Judge Broderick: Jurors, consider whether to discuss what happened in the jury room. You are now excused. I will come back and thank each of you.

And afterward, the SDNY prosecutors "announced that a jury was unable to reach a unanimous decision as to whether to authorize the death penalty for SAYFULLO SAIPOV. U.S. District Judge Vernon S. Broderick will sentence SAIPOV to the statutorily mandated sentence of life in prison."

It ends with a whimper, not a bang. But Saipov was quoted during the trial that he believes he survived because big things await him.

At this Kurt perked up. He and Michael Randall Long would stay on the case(s)

www.ingramcontent.com/pod-product-compliance
Lightning Source LLC
Chambersburg PA
CBHW071136220526
45467CB00015B/1128